IARIA

ICONS 2017

The Twelfth International Conference on Systems

April 23 - 27, 2017

Venice, Italy

ICONS 2017 Editors

Mark Austin, University of Maryland at College Park, USA
Andrew Snow, Ohio University, USA
Fabrice Mourlin, U-PEC University, France

Printed from e-media with permission by:

Curran Associates, Inc.
57 Morehouse Lane
Red Hook, NY 12571

Some format issues inherent in the e-media version may also appear in this print version.

Printed by Curran Associates, Inc. (2017)

International Academy, Research, and Industry Association (IARIA)
412 Derby Way
Wilmington, DE 19810

Phone: (408) 893-6407
Fax: (408) 527-6351

petre@iaria.org

Additional copies of this publication are available from:

Curran Associates, Inc.
57 Morehouse Lane
Red Hook, NY 12571 USA
Phone: 845-758-0400
Fax: 845-758-2633
Email: curran@proceedings.com
Web: www.proceedings.com

TABLE OF CONTENTS

ICONS 1: ADVANCED SYSTEMS

ICONS 2 / EVSYS: EVOLVING SYSTEMS

ICONS 3: APPLICATION-ORIENTED SYSTEMS

ICONS 2017

Forward

The Twelfth International Conference on Systems (ICONS 2017), held between April 23-27, 2017 in Venice, Italy, continued a series of events covering a broad spectrum of topics. The conference covered fundamentals on designing, implementing, testing, validating and maintaining various kinds of software and hardware systems. Several tracks were proposed to treat the topics from theory to practice, in terms of methodologies, design, implementation, testing, use cases, tools, and lessons learnt.

In the past years, new system concepts have been promoted and partially embedded in new deployments. Anticipative systems, autonomic and autonomous systems, self-adapting systems, or on-demand systems are systems exposing advanced features. These features demand special requirements specification mechanisms, advanced behavioral design patterns, special interaction protocols, and flexible implementation platforms. Additionally, they require new monitoring and management paradigms, as self-protection, self-diagnosing, self-maintenance become core design features.

The design of application-oriented systems is driven by application-specific requirements that have a very large spectrum. Despite the adoption of uniform frameworks and system design methodologies supported by appropriate models and system specification languages, the deployment of application-oriented systems raises critical problems. Specific requirements in terms of scalability, realtime, security, performance, accuracy, distribution, and user interaction drive the design decisions and implementations. This leads to the need for gathering application-specific knowledge and develop particular design and implementation skills that can be reused in developing similar systems.

Validation and verification of safety requirements for complex systems containing hardware, software and human subsystems must be considered from early design phases. There is a need for rigorous analysis on the role of people and process causing hazards within safety-related systems; however, these claims are often made without a rigorous analysis of the human factors involved. Accurate identification and implementation of safety requirements for all elements of a system, including people and procedures become crucial in complex and critical systems, especially in safety related projects from the civil aviation, defense health, and transport sectors.

Fundamentals on safety-related systems concern both positive (desired properties) and negative (undesired properties) aspects. Safety requirements are expressed at the individual equipment level and at the operational-environment level. However, ambiguity in safety requirements may lead to reliable unsafe systems. Additionally, the distribution of safety requirements between people and machines makes difficult automated proofs of system safety. This is somehow obscured by the difficulty of applying formal techniques (usually used for equipment-related safety requirements) to derivation and satisfaction of human-related safety requirements (usually, human factors techniques are used).

The conference had the following tracks:

- Advanced systems
- Application-oriented systems
- EVSYS: Evolving Systems

We take here the opportunity to warmly thank all the members of the ICONS 2017 technical program committee, as well as all the reviewers. The creation of such a high quality conference program would not have been possible without their involvement. We also kindly thank all the authors that dedicated much of their time and effort to contribute to ICONS 2017. We truly believe that, thanks to all these efforts, the final conference program consisted of top quality contributions.

We also gratefully thank the members of the ICONS 2017 organizing committee for their help in handling the logistics and for their work that made this professional meeting a success.

We hope that ICONS 2017 was a successful international forum for the exchange of ideas and results between academia and industry and to promote further progress in the field of systems. We also hope that Venice, Italy provided a pleasant environment during the conference and everyone saved some time to enjoy the unique charm of the city.

ICONS 2017 Committee

ICONS Steering Committee

Marko Jäntti, University of Eastern Finland, Finland
Leszek Koszalka, Wroclaw University of Technology, Poland
Mark Austin, University of Maryland at College Park, USA
Zoubir Mammeri, IRIT - Paul Sabatier University, France
Raimund Ege, Northern Illinois University, USA
Andrew Snow, Ohio University, USA

ICONS Industry/Research Advisory Committee

Gary Weckman, Ohio University, USA
Tzung-Pei Hong [洪宗貝], National University of Kaohsiung, Taiwan

ICONS 2017
Committee

ICONS Steering Committee

Marko Jäntti, University of Eastern Finland, Finland
Leszek Koszalka, Wroclaw University of Technology, Poland
Mark Austin, University of Maryland at College Park, USA
Zoubir Mammeri, IRIT - Paul Sabatier University, France
Raimund Ege, Northern Illinois University, USA
Andrew Snow, Ohio University, USA

ICONS Industry/Research Advisory Committee

Gary Weckman, Ohio University, USA
Tzung-Pei Hong [洪宗貝], National University of Kaohsiung, Taiwan

ICONS 2017 Technical Program Committee

Mehmud Abliz, Google Inc., USA
Mehmet Aksit, University of Twente, Netherlands
Mark Austin, University of Maryland at College Park, USA
Lubomir Bakule, Institute of Information Theory and Automation of the CAS, Czech Republic
Zbigniew Banaszak, Technical University of Koszalin, Poland
Ateet Bhalla, Independent Consultant, India
Francesco Bianconi, University of Perugia, Italy
Isabelle Borne, University of South Brittany | IRISA Laboratory, France
Albert M. K. Cheng, University of Houston, USA
David Cordeau, University of Poitiers, France
Peter De Bruyn, University of Antwerp, Belgium
Bayram Deviren, Nevsehir Hacı Bektas Veli University, Turkey
Yezyd Donoso, Universidad de los Andes - Bogotá, Colombia
Raimund Ege, Northern Illinois University, USA
Andras Farago, University of Texas at Dallas, USA
Francesco Fontanella, Università di Cassino e del Lazio meridionale, Italy
Miguel Franklin de Castro, Federal University of Ceará, Brazil
Marta Franova, CNRS, LRI & INRIA, Orsay, France
Matthias Galster, University of Canterbury, Christchurch, New Zealand
Christos Gatzidis, Bournemouth University, UK
Patrick Girard, LIRMM / CNRS, France
Frederic Guinand, Normandy University (Le Havre), France / Cardinal Stefan Wyszynski University in Warsaw, Poland

Tzung-Pei Hong, National University of Kaohsiung, Taiwan
Michael Hübner, Ruhr-University of Bochum, Germany
Wen-Jyi Hwang, National Taiwan Normal University, Taiwan
Tomasz Hyla, West Pomeranian University of Technology, Szczecin, Poland
Marko Jäntti, University of Eastern Finland, Finland
Hermann Kaindl, Vienna University of Technology, Austria
Fu-Chien Kao, Da-Yeh University, Taiwan
Andrzej Kasprzak, Wroclaw University of Technology, Poland
Leszek Koszalka, Wroclaw University of Science and Technology, Poland
Wim Laurier, Université Saint-Louis / Ghent University, Belgium
Suzanne Lesecq, Commissariat à l'énergie atomique et aux énergies alternatives (CEA), France
David Lizcano Casas, Open University of Madrid (UDIMA), Spain
Ivan Lukovic, University of Novi Sad, Serbia
Jia-Ning Luo, Ming Chuan University, Taiwan
Stephane Maag, Institut Mines-Telecom / Telecom SudParis, France
Avinash Malik, University of Auckland, New Zealand
Zoubir Mammeri, IRIT - Paul Sabatier University, France
D. Manivannan, University of Kentucky, USA
Michele Melchiori, Università degli Studi di Brescia, Italy
Fernando Moreira, Universidade Portucalense, Portugal
Fabrice Mourlin, UPEC University, France
Timothy W. O'Neil, The University of Akron, USA
Joanna Isabelle Olszewska, University of Gloucestershire, UK
Flavio Oquendo, IRISA - University of South Brittany, France
Przemyslaw (Pshemek) Pawluk, George Brown College Toronto, Canada
George Perry, University of Texas at San Antonio, USA
Marta Piekarska, Technical University of Berlin, Germany
Iwona Pozniak-Koszalka, Wroclaw University of Science and Technology, Poland
Grzegorz Redlarski, Gdansk University of Technology, Poland
José Ignacio Rojas Sola, University of Jaén, Spain
Juha Röning, University of Oulu, Finland
Francesca Saglietti, Universität Erlangen-Nürnberg, Germany
Sebastien Salva, UCA (University Clermont Auvergne), LIMOS, France
Elisa Schaeffer, Universidad Autónoma de Nuevo León, Mexico
Rainer Schönbein, Fraunhofer Institute of Optronics, System Technologies and Image Exploitation (IOSB), Germany
Zary Segall, University of Maryland Baltimore County, USA
Yilun Shang, Tongji University, China
Charlie Y. Shim, Kutztown University of Pennsylvania, USA
Andrew Snow, Ohio University, USA
Pedro Sousa, University of Minho, Portugal
Agnieszka Szczęsna, Silesian University of Technology, Poland
Yoshiaki Taniguchi, Kindai University, Japan
Anel Tanovic, University of Sarajevo, Bosnia and Herzegovina

Copyright Information

Performance of Authenticated Encryption for Payment Cards with Crypto Co-processors

Keith Mayes

Royal Holloway, University of London
Egham, Surrey, UK
Email: keith.mayes@rhul.ac.uk

***Abstract*—Many security protocols rely on authentication of communicating entities and encryption of exchanged data. Traditionally, authentication and encryption have been separate processes, however there are combined solutions, referred to as authenticated-encryption (AE). The payment card industry is revising its protocol specifications and considering AE, however there has been uncertainty around performance and feasibility on traditional issued smart cards and when loaded as applications on security chips pre-installed within devices. It is difficult to predict performance using results from generic CPUs as typical smart card chips used in payment, have slow CPUs yet fast crypto-coprocessors. This report is based on a practical investigation, commissioned by a standards body, that compared secure platform level (MULTOS) and low-level native implementations of AE on crypto-coprocessor smart cards. The work also suggests a technology independent benchmark for a CPU with crypto-coprocessor.**

Keywords–Authenticated encryption; EMV; OCB; GCM; ETM; CCM; smart card; crypto-coprocessor; payment; performance; MULTOS.

I. Introduction

The EMVCo organisation [4] developed the Europay, Mastercard and Visa (EMV) standards [3] that affect billions of payment smart cards. The cards use secured microcontroller chips, designed to be strongly tamper-resistant and independently evaluated to Common Criteria (CC) [2] levels of at least Evaluation Assurance Level (EAL)4+. Despite strong defensive capabilities, the chips lag behind the state-of-the-art in CPU performance and memory sizes. However, despite these limitations the chips excel in cryptographic operations as they incorporate relatively high-speed crypto-coprocessor hardware. The EMVCo organisation is reviewing the use of Authenticated Encryption (AE) [10] for future payment card processing. There are a number of potential modes and those originally of interest included Offset Codebook (OCB) [15], Galois Counter Mode (GCM) [20], Counter with Cipher Block Chaining Message Authentication Code (CCM) [19] and Encrypt-then-MAC (ETM) [10]. Within this study, GCM was eventually substituted for OCB3 as the former required binary field multiplication, which was not supported by the available crypto-coprocessors. There have been previous studies of AE performance, however they have generally focussed on more powerful generic CPUs, without dedicated crypto-coprocessors. As a starting point we take the study by Krovetz and Rogaway [14], which shows that OCB performance is faster (for the given test conditions) than alternatives; however there are several reasons why these results cannot be immediately accepted as relevant for EMV protocols:

- The command messages in traditional smart cards are small; the data field restricted to 255 bytes; larger payloads accommodated by multiple messages.
- The results do not adequately address the case of a slow CPU with a relatively fast crypto-coprocessor.
- Support for Associated Data is not required.
- Smart cards have very restricted memory sizes with different write speeds for Random Access Memory (RAM) and Non-Volatile Memory (NVM).
- Conventional smart card interfaces are quite slow and so protocols can be communication limited rather than processing limited.

In order to gain a better appreciation of the comparative performance of AE on realistic smart card platforms, a practical study was initiated, considering first a secure platform implementation (MULTOS) [17] and then a native mode equivalent. This report describes the experimental requirements in Section II and then gives an overview of the AE modes in Section III. The platform and native results are presented and discussed in Sections IV and V respectively. Section VI discusses how implementation security may affect performance measurements, and Section VII considers communication limitations. Conclusions and suggestions for future work are presented in Section VIII.

II. Experimental Requirements

The study investigated comparative performance of AE modes implemented in both a secured smart card application platform (representative of a pre-deployed device), and as native code on a smart card chip. The selected platform was a MULTOS ML3 card, using the Infineon SLE78 chip [7], which can be CC EAL4+ certified, and includes good defences against physical, side-channel [12][13] and fault attacks. The native mode implementation used a Samsung 16-bit smart card chip (S3CC9E8) [23], and as the crypto-coprocessor did not support AES, its performance comparisons used 3DES/DES [5]. The S3CC9E8 is a secured microcontroller with physical attack protection, fault sensors and some side-channel countermeasures, however it would normally require added defensive measures in software; this is discussed further in Section VI. The AE modes considered in detail were OCB (OCB2 and OCB3), CCM and ETM; with some GCM experiments.

The EMV protocol would normally have a preliminary Diffie Hellman key and nonce exchange, however this was not modelled as would be common to all AE modes and so would not affect performance comparison. Associated Data is not needed in the EMV protocol. Communicated data is required to fit within one or more standard Application Data Protocol Units (APDU) [8], and with the exception of OCB modes, all APDU payloads that are not multiples of the encryption block-size are padded prior to encryption. The memory in smart card chips is very restricted and protocol/algorithm execution is expected to place very limited demands on it, leaving maximum space for OS and applications. For our tests, a working assumption was that 80-90% of the memory was unavailable. The RAM in smart cards is usually much faster for writing than the NVM and so critical objects/buffers are implemented in a RAM. Our application was limited to no more than 10% of the available RAM (so if 8k, we could have 800 bytes). The application was restricted to no more than 10% of the available code/data space (so if a 64k flash device then 6.4kbytes was allowed). Some implementations benefit from trading NVM space for speed using pre-computed tables, which is not well suited to smart cards, but up to 10% of the NVM space was assumed available for this. In general the imposed memory restrictions proved not to be a problem for the implemented AE modes.

Test software was in 'C', so it could be adapted and directly comparable for both MULTOS and native implementations. There is a single test application that incorporates all the AE modes plus test utilities that measure various core functions. The interface is based on APDU commands and responses, with the payload data consisting of blocks of plaintext or ciphertext. For message timing precision, commands were run 1024 times before response, in order to compensate for measurement tolerance. Communication delay was removed (via calibration) from the test results, although it is reconsidered in Section VII. We will now continue the discussion by providing an overview of the AE modes.

III. Overview of Authenticated Encryption Modes

Offset Codebook mode is defined as mechanism 1 in ISO/IEC 19772 [10] and is also described in RFC 7253[15]. The principles of operation are also well presented on Phil Rogaway's website [21]. For convenience, we will summarise the basic operations of OCB2 here. In Figure 1, an initialisation vector is first computed and then the plaintext message is split into blocks (M1-3, M* in example), all but the last block must be the size of the block cipher, so for AES128 we have 128 bit blocks. They are then encrypted (with modification from the input vector) to produce ciphertext blocks. The complete output is the sequence of C1-3, C* plus an extra value T. Note that because of a requirement to recompute the intialisation vector, this AE is most optimum for a 64 block message sequence and least optimum for a single block message.

CCM is mechanism 3 in ISO/IEC19772[10] and described in NIST SP800-38C[19] and [24]. Figure 2 overviews CCM operation. Whilst the simplified diagram just shows a nonce/-counter input to the stages of the MAC calculation, the generic standard description also specifies some flag/length bit fields.

ETM scheme (see Figure 3) is mechanism 5 in ISO/IEC 19772 [10], and is a conventional approach with separate

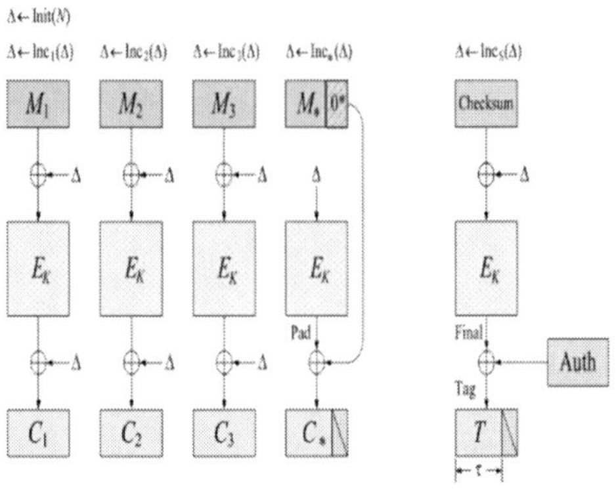

Figure 1. OCB with Incomplete Blocks [Rogaway]

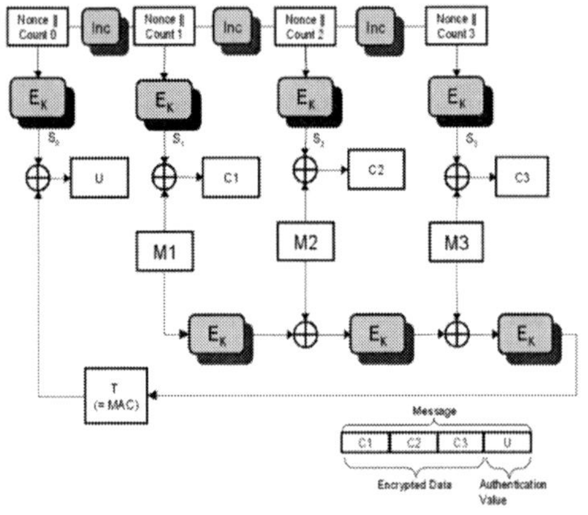

Figure 2. CCM Overview (simplified)

encryption and MAC processes. It does not support Associated Data, although this is not required for the study. The encryption stage uses block encryption in counter mode with key K, followed by a MAC computation on the cipher text using a different key (K') to that used for encryption. According to ISO/IEC 19772[10] the MAC algorithm is selected from the ISO/IEC 9797 standards [11], in which there are six different MAC options, all of which have numerous variants. The selected options for the tests are listed below.

- MAC Algorithm: 1 (usually referred to as CBC-MAC)
- Padding Method: 1 (zeros)
- Final Iteration: 1 (same as other iterations)
- Output Transformation: 1 (unity = no change)
- Truncation: - (left most 64 bits)

GCM (see Figure 4) mode of operation is mechanism 6 in ISO/IEC 19772 [10] and also described in NIST SP800-38D [20] and [22]. The performance of this mode could not be very usefully compared using the traditional crypto-coprocessors used for the study as GCM requires support for multiplication over Galois Field GF (2^{128}) with the hash key H, which is the encryption of all zeros under E_K.

A. *Workload Estimation*

Table I gives an indication of the underlying workload for each mode when processing the representative test message sizes (as advised by the commissioning standards body).

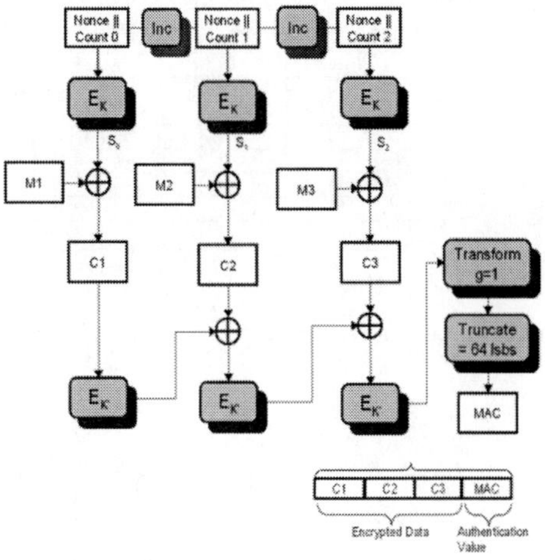

Figure 3. Encrypt then MAC

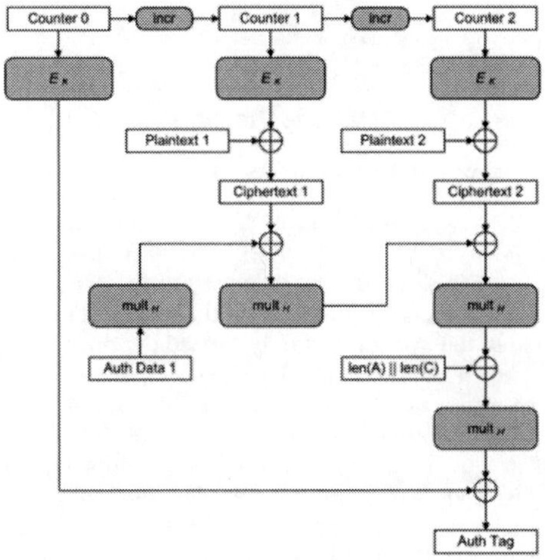

Figure 4. CCM Overview (simplified)

IV. Platform Mode Results

For security, certification and reliability reasons, it is not normal to have native code access to a smart card or similar security chip once deployed. Instead the chip may offer a secure platform where added functionality is constrained to a tightly controlled application layer, using APIs to access security capabilities. The MULTOS card is such a secure platform whereby the application execution language is abstracted from the underlying hardware (see [18]), offering high standards of security, but making it difficult to predict performance of the core AE functionality. The results of initial benchmark tests

TABLE I. ALGORITHM WORKLOAD PER MODE

Bytes	Blks	Msgs	OCB		GCM		CCM	ETM
			E	Init	E	Mul	E	E
8	1	1	3	1	2	2	3	2
16	1	1	3	1	2	2	3	2
20	2	1	4	1	3	3	5	4
32	2	1	4	1	3	3	5	4
40	3	1	5	1	4	4	7	6
64	4	1	6	1	5	5	9	8
128	8	1	10	1	9	9	17	16
192	12	1	14	1	13	13	25	24

TABLE II. MULTOS BENCHMARK MEASUREMENTS (ms)

Function	Primitive		Application		Used
	RAM	NVM	RAM	NVM	
Block Encrypt	3.3	6.4			3.3
Block Xor	0.73	3.94	3.21	15.84	0.73
Block Shift	1.24		2.7		1.24
Block Copy	0.36		0.65		0.36
GF Multiply			199		199

are shown in Table II.

The time measured for a block encrypt with a 128-bit key was 3.3ms (confirmed by MULTOS as matching in-house results). The underlying chip crypto-engine is much faster, and the speed disparity is due to software reliability and security measures. The 3.3ms is only valid when writing encrypted data to RAM, as NVM increases the time to 6.4ms (although reading from NVM is fast); so the outputs of all functions were written to RAM. In all cases where a primitive was available, it was considerably quicker than any equivalent implemented at the application layer, although considerably slower than what might be imagined from a low-level native implementation

GCM requires a finite field multiply, but such a function did not exist as a MULTOS primitive and so was provided in a simple implementation similar to *Algorithm 1* in the standard [16]. Multiplying a single block takes 199ms, even when using primitives *multosBlockShiftRight* and *MultosBlockXor*. Other implementations are described in the standard, although they make use of time/memory trade-offs, which is not a strength for a memory limited smart card. For the initial tests, all the modes and the extra test utilities were built into a single application with the following memory requirements.

- Code Size (NVM): 5701 bytes
- Static Data (NVM): 498 bytes
- Session Data (RAM): 113 bytes

All the sizes are well within the realistic and practical design targets defined at the start of the project. For a single mode application the code size would be considerably less, and the static data is mainly internally stored test-vectors that would not normally be present. The session data could be reduced, if required.

A. *Initial Tests and Optimisation*

Following the MULTOS benchmark tests, the GCM mode was removed from the study (on request of the commissioning standards body) and more attention given to OCB (version 2) optimisation; and later OCB3 was also added. GCM requires specialist hardware support that was not available from the crypto-coprocessors in the test chips, whereas the other AE modes could be implemented in a straightforward manner. OCB2 was initially implemented from the published example code (see Figure 5)that was critically dependent on a function called *two_times()*.

This was replaced with a version (with less shifts) more suited to the MULTOS Platform (see Figure 6), which had a marked improvement on performance.

Given the resulting speed-up (four/five times on larger messages) from improving OCB2 code, it was decided to also implement OCB3 based on the pseudo code and test vectors in RFC7253 [14].

```
//128-bit shift-left src <<= 1, XOR 0x87 if carry out
{unsigned i;
unsigned char carry=src[0]>>7;
// carry = high bit of src
for (i=0; i<sizeof(block)-1; i++) {
  dst[i]=(src[i]<<1)|(src[i+1]>>7); }
  dst[sizeof(block)-1]=(src[sizeof(block)-1]<<1)
                        ^(carry*0x87);
  }
```

Figure 5. Published Example Code for *two_times()*

```
static void two_times(block dst, block src)
{
 unsigned char carry = src[0] & 0x80;
 multosBlockShiftLeft(AES_BLK_SZ, 1, src, src);
 if (carry) {src[AES_BLK_SZ - 1] ^= 0x87;}
 }
```

Figure 6. MULTOS Code for *two_times()*

1) OCB3 Memory considerations: At the beginning of the OCB3 encrypt pseudo code, a number of bit arrays need to be set-up, see Figure 7, noting that '_' is used to indicate subscript in the pseudo code and that *double()* is the same as the *two_times()* function used in OCB2. The array L_i to use in block processing, varies per message block using index L_[*ntz(i)*]. **L_i:** If we allow for processing 64 blocks of 128

```
L_* = ENCIPHER(K, zeros(128))
L_$ = double(L_*)
L_0 = double(L_$)
L_i = double(L_{i-1}) for every integer i > 0
```

Figure 7. OCB3 Key-dependent Variable Set-up

bits then it might appear that we need 64 of the L_i arrays. However the *ntz(i)* index means we only need 6 ($2^6 = 64$) L_i arrays, as well as L_*, L_$ and L_0. Therefore we need 9 blocks (144 bytes), rather than 67 blocks; which is well within our target RAM limit.

ntz(): Another memory requirement arises from the ntz() function. Bit/byte manipulations at the MULTOS application layer are slow and so it is quicker to implement the function as a look up table. For a maximum 64 block message we require a 64 byte array that can be precomputed and stored in NVM. This small amount of memory is easily accommodated within a smart card.

2) OCB3 Functional Aspects: OCB3 defines a hash function for use with Associated Data, however this is not needed in the EMV experiments. OCB3 has a preparation stage where key and nonce related data is readied prior to processing message blocks. The key data was described earlier (computation is relatively straight forward) and nonce related data is illustrated in Figure 8. This is mostly straightforward apart from the innocuous looking line showing the calculation of *Offset_0*. The variable *bottom* will have a value between 0 and 63; and it is effectively used as a bit-wise left shift. As discovered

```
Nonce = num2str(TAGLEN mod 128,7)
        ||zeros(120-bitlen(N))||1||N
bottom = str2num(Nonce[123..128])
Ktop = ENCIPHER(K, Nonce[1..122]||zeros(6))
Stretch = Ktop||(Ktop[1..64] xor Ktop[9..72])
Offset_0 = Stretch[1+bottom..128+bottom]
Checksum_0 = zeros(128)
```

Figure 8. OCB3 Nonce and Pre-encrypt Variables

TABLE III. MULTOS PLATFORM RESULTS (ms)

Bytes	OCB2	CCM	ETM	OCB3
8	16.59	17.78	14.27	28.66
16	16.61	17.22	13.70	29.27
20	22.17	25.73	22.21	34.40
32	22.17	25.16	21.62	35.00
40	27.72	33.67	30.15	40.12
64	33.35	41.09	37.57	46.42
128	55.77	72.91	69.38	69.21
192	78.17	104.73	101.22	92.06

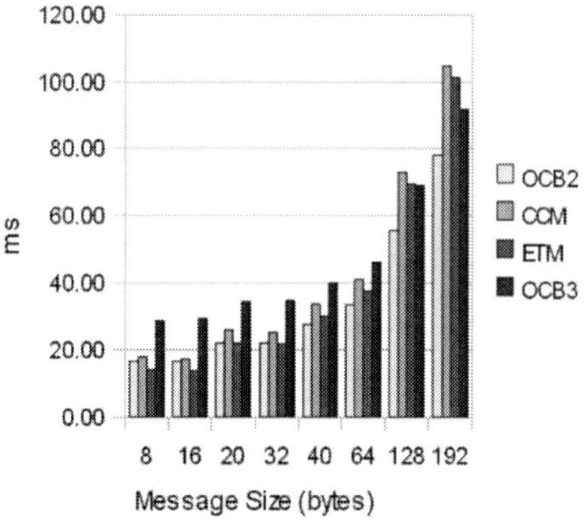

Figure 9. AE Comparative Performance on MULTOS Platform

previously, application level bit-shifts are inefficient on the MULTOS test platform, however the primitives *multosBlockShiftLeft/Right* are much quicker. Unfortunately, the primitives require a fixed constant value for the number of places to shift. Although the operation is only carried out once per message it could adversely affect efficiency, especially of small messages and so effort was directed towards optimisation. The first step was to split *bottom* into a number of byte shifts plus a smaller number (up to seven) bit shifts. Byte shifts are easy as we can just change the array index. The bit-shifts were used in a switch/case to reach primitive calls with the appropriate number of shifts. More code was needed, but the overall code space requirements are small.

B. MULTOS Platform Results

The results from testing OCB2, CCM, ETM and OCB3 are shown in Table III.

From the MULTOS results we can see OCB2 is the quickest mode for message sizes beyond 32bytes. OCB3's initial processing makes it slower than OCB2, and OCB3 only overtakes ETM for messages larger than 128 bytes. CCM is always a little slower than ETM due to the extra encryption block, and both are less efficient when working on input data that requires padding.

Although OCB2 seems the faster option for the MULTOS platform (for messages 32+bytes) the relative difference in processing time is not enormous. OCB2 benefited from some optimisation, however there is little scope for improvement in ETM and CCM as much of their time is spent encrypting, which is only possible via a MULTOS API call. The MULTOS platform (and platforms in general) add abstraction between the application layer and the underlying hardware, and so there is considerable uncertainty that the comparative results of Table III would be similar in a native mode smart card implementation. Furthermore, the absolute performance

TABLE IV. TDES MASKED MODE AE TIMES (ms)

Bytes	OCB2	CCM	ETM	OCB3
8	3.04	2.16	1.53	5.75
16	3.07	2.12	1.49	5.81
20	4.19	3.48	2.85	6.73
32	4.24	3.43	2.80	6.81
40	5.37	4.77	4.15	7.76
64	6.57	6.04	5.42	8.81
128	11.23	11.28	10.65	12.82
192	15.89	16.51	15.89	16.82

times on the MULTOS platform, would be expected to be at least one order of magnitude slower than a simple native implementation. Therefore, the AE modes were next tested on a hardware emulator for an older, but still relevant 16-bit smart card chip (Samsung S3CC9E8).

V. Native Mode

Obtaining a native mode hardware emulator for a "real" smart card with crypto-coprocessor (for use in academic research) is not trivial and only the S3CC9E8 emulator/chip was suitable and used in payment cards; although because it did not support AES, substitute 16 byte block encryption functions were needed. To ensure that comparative performance results would be relevant to standards, the commissioning standards body was consulted on the substitutes. The AES 16byte data block was considered as a pair of 8byte data blocks (M1 and M2) to be coded with DES or triple DES (TDES), i.e., TDES(M1)||(M2) or DES(M1)||(M2). Clearly these functions were for performance evaluation only, although TDES(M1)||TDES(M2) was also coded as a more secure, but overly co-processor intensive alternative.

A. Initial Implementation and Measurement

This stage was focussed on porting the MULTOS code to the native emulator and generating early raw results for functional checking. They derive from non-optimised code, simply replacing the MULTOS primitive calls with equivalents. The performance of the AE modes (including OCB3) was measured in a similar way to the MULTOS work. The first tests used the dual TDES(M1)||TDES(M2) block encryption option (hardest to compute) and the results are in Table IV.

From these initial native results, we observe that the processing time for a single message was under 17ms, regardless of the AE mode. Although the block ciphers were of course different, the overall native execution times were significantly faster than those from the MULTOS experiments, even without optimisation. ETM was the best option for single APDU messages, although in absolute terms there was not much to choose between any of the modes. For smaller messages, ETM and CCM still seemed to have the advantage over the OCB modes. Common to both native and MULTOS implementations ETM is always a little better than CCM and OCB3 does not seem to improve on OCB2.

B. Optimisations

The original source code used within the initial tests was very similar to the MULTOS code. The scope for optimisation on the MULTOS platform was limited as core functions were most efficiently carried out using platform primitives that were abstracted from the underlying hardware. Native mode programming generally offers more opportunity for optimisation as there is less hardware abstraction. Only speed optimisation was considered in this part of the study as all versions of the native code were well within our target memory bounds.

TABLE V. OPTIMISATION OF CORE FUNCTION EXECUTION (ms)

Function	Original	Optimised
Block Xor	0.161	0.071
Block Copy	0.114	0.064
ECB TDES || TDES + mask	0.608	0.381
Fixed Block Shift Left	0.330	0.073

Data Block Copy and XOR: The algorithm modes make use of simple byte manipulation functions including XOR and Copy. In the MULTOS implementation these functions were provided by MULTOS primitives, which in the native code were initially replaced by simple equivalents that assumed variable sized fields and handled data byte-by-byte. However, within the authentication modes, very few operations use variable sized fields, with the majority working on 16 byte memory blocks. Knowing the field size, means that we can avoid loop counters, and by ensuring that the blocks are aligned on 4-byte boundaries we can perform operations on unsigned long integer types rather than bytes. Referring to Table V we see that as a result, BlockXor and BlockCopy have almost doubled in speed, which has also improved the overall block cipher performance. Note that functional calls are still used at this stage rather than in-line code.

Block Shifts: The OCB modes use Copy and XOR operations, but also rely on the function *two_times()* (discussed earlier), which in turn makes use of a function for shifting the contents of a block to the left. The function from the first tests, *BlockShiftLeft()* was a direct replacement for the MULTOS primitive that supported variable shifts on variable sized blocks, referred to by pointer parameters. However, in practice, *two_times()* can be constrained to always use shifts of one place in a 16 byte global variable block. It was therefore possible to create a simpler *FixBlockShiftLeft()* function to use instead. The resulting speed improvement for the shift functions was very significant, as shown in Table V.

Further Refinement: When implementing the block cipher functions, further optimisation removed calls to core functions involving variable length arguments, and in some cases replaced them with simple in-line code. The block encryption function no longer called the core functions, but had faster in-line equivalents. The different block functions are handled by compile-time switches. Note that when using a crypto-coprocessor an input may be masked to reduce side-channel leakage and so a dummy mask was included in the test modes. An option was also added to clear the keys after use, however this was not used in the main measurements. The extended set of benchmarked measurements is shown in Table VI, however now that operations are speed optimised the absolute figures are significantly influenced by the measurement command handling. It is more useful to consider the relative measurements, e.g., by subtracting the FixBlockCopy time from the others.

C. Native Mode Results

Following the additional optimisations, the message tests were repeated for the substitute block cipher function TDES(M1)||M2. The functions are clearly intended to assess performance, rather than to ensure security of the data. The results are provided in Table VII and shown graphically in Figure 10.

TABLE VI. OPTIMISED CORE PERFORMANCE BENCHMARKS (ms)

Functionality	Time
FixBlockXor	0.071
FixBlockCopy	0.064
FixBlockShiftLeft	0.073
DES(M1)||M2	0.128
DES(M1)||DES(M2)	0.141
DES(M1)||DES(M2) + mask XOR	0.146
DES(M1)||DES(M2) + mask XOR + key clear	0.154
TDES(M1)||M2	0.140
TDES(M1)||TDES(M2)	0.163
TDES(M1)||TDES(M2) + mask XOR	0.169
TDES(M1)||TDES(M2) + mask XOR + key clear	0.178

TABLE VII. TDES(M1)||M2 AE TIMES (ms)

Bytes	OCB2	CCM	ETM	OCB3
8	0.54	0.34	0.27	0.83
16	0.57	0.30	0.23	0.79
20	0.65	0.50	0.43	0.92
32	0.70	0.45	0.38	0.91
40	0.79	0.64	0.57	1.07
64	0.95	0.75	0.68	1.16
128	1.46	1.35	1.28	1.65
192	1.96	1.95	1.88	2.14

D. Observations on the Native Tests

Considering Table VI we have significantly improved the performance of core functions. We can also use these results to estimate the achievable raw speed of the crypto-coprocessor, by cancelling out the software manipulations. For both DES and TDES operations we set-up the same keys (two are redundant for DES, but help our timing comparison), wrote in the input data once and read out the result once. The DES crypto-engine overwrites its input data with its output and so for TDES the CPU does not need to move data between the sequence of DES executions; it just refers to a different pre-stored key for each execution. Therefore, if we look at the times for an equivalent DES and TDES operation the difference should be the time taken for the extra DES executions. This time is largely dependent on the hardware although the execution has to be started and checked for completion by the CPU. We can estimate the core DES run time t_d using the following example, where $t(f)$ is the time to execute function f.

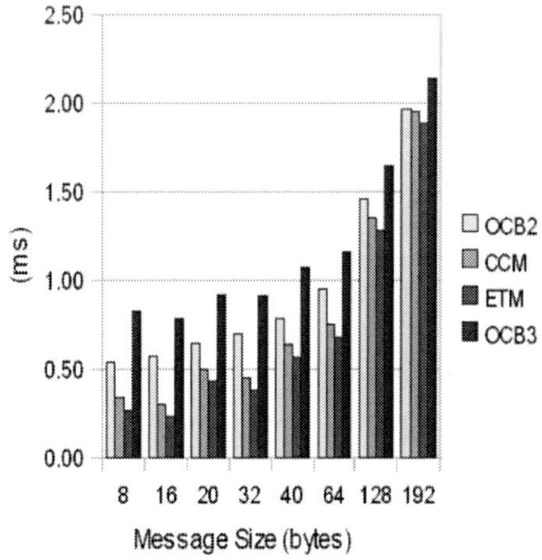

Figure 10. Optimised TDES(M1)||M2 AE Times (ms)

$$\begin{aligned} 2t_d &= t(TDES(M1)||M2) - t(DES(M1)||M2) \\ &= 0.140 - 0.128 \\ &= 0.012ms \end{aligned} \tag{1}$$

There were two extra DES runs in the TDES version so we might suppose that each was about 6us. We can check this by calculating the following.

$$\begin{aligned} 4t_d &= t(TDES(M1)||TDES(M2)) \\ &\quad - t(DES(M1)||DES(M2)) \\ &= 0.163 - 0.141 \\ &= 0.022ms \end{aligned} \tag{2}$$

The four extra DES runs take 22us, about 5.5us each; which is close to our earlier estimate. We can also see from Table VI that the dummy XOR on a 16byte block using in-line code takes about the same time, 5-6us. The key-clear, which is a 24 byte write, takes about 8-9us, so a 16byte block copy should be in a similar 5-6us range. The optimisations improved the speed of all AE modes.

E. Technology Independent Gain Assessment

Generally the native mode results demonstrated that for the particular chip, the crypto-coprocessor could execute its main block cipher in about the same time as the simplest of CPU functions (XOR) on a similar sized block. This could be defined as say the Technology Independent Gain Assessment (TIGA) for any CPU with a crypto-coprocessor. It could be expressed as the percentage of the block encryption that can be completed by the crypto-coprocessor in the time it would take the CPU to compute a block XOR; in our native case this would be 100% and 33% respectively for DES and TDES. In the case of a platform, the benchmark would be computed from the API measurements as we are restricted to the application level. Referring back to the MULTOS measurements in Table II then the TIGA benchmark figure would be approximately 22%. Although we are not comparing like-with-like block ciphers due to practical experimental restrictions, TIGA is at least a means to make comparison. A high figure would suggest that a designer could use block encryptions as readily as XORs and so algorithm optimisation and performance would be quite different to conventional (non crypro-coprocessor) CPUs.

At this point it should be recalled that cards/chips of interest are security sensitive and likely to be attacked. Fortunately countermeasures are quite well understood by the card industry, but they can potentially impact on performance, and so in the next section we consider how our results might be affected.

VI. Implementation Security and Performance

Payment cards safeguard financial transactions of significant value and so are required to strongly resist a wide range of attacks. EMV cards rely on the protection of various stored assets including cryptographic keys, account details and PINs, as well as on the integrity of critical functionality Adhering to information security best practice guidelines for design, (e.g., for algorithms, keys and random number generation) is not at all sufficient as many of the attacks target the implementation rather than the design. In smart cards, the attack resistance will be provided by a mix of hardware and software measures and so there is potential for performance impact. We can consider such attacks under the following three categories.

- Physical
- Fault
- Side-Channel

A. Physical Attack Resistance

Physical attack generally requires considerable expertise, equipment and time. It may for example involve decapsulating a chip, hardware reverse engineering, probing buses and memories and modifying tracks. However smart card chips have numerous defences against such intrusions, including:

- Passive and active shields - to prevent access to a working chip
- Encrypted buses and memories - to impede direct probing
- Light sensors - to detect decapsulation
- Scrambled circuit layout - to make hardware reverse engineering difficult

Both the chips used in this study incorporate these protective measures, and because they are inherent in the hardware we do not need to degrade our performance test results.

B. Fault Attack Resistance

Fault attacks are active, in that they use means to disrupt the normal operation of the target device (chip); but without damaging it. The faults can, for example, be generated from voltage glitches, radiation pulses and operating the target outside of its operational specification. Under fault conditions the chip may reveal all kinds of information that it would not do when working normally and there are some very elegant attacks including extraction of RSA keys [1]. The hardware sensors in traditional tamper-resistant smart cards (like the S3CC9E8) are intended to detect the likely means of fault insertion and prevent a response useful to the attacker; so there may be no significant added overhead for the software. A sophisticated attack might possibly bypass the sensors, however by adopting openly peer-reviewed algorithms and using diversified card keys, we remove motivation for such effort. Added countermeasures could be to verify a result or to run an algorithm twice and only output a response if the result is valid/consistent, however both strategies rely on the correct outcomes of flag tests and loop counts. It is therefore good practice to add defensive coding of loop and flag tests, at the cost of some additional processing overhead,

The SLE78 chip works very differently to a traditional smart card chip as it has two CPUs working in tandem and a fault is detected if their processing does not agree. This is an innovative and effective approach, which would make it very difficult to succeed with a fault attack. As the protection is inherent in the chip hardware it should not noticeably impact our test results.

C. Side-Channel Attack Resistance

Side-channel leakage implies the leakage of sensitive information (especially keys) via an unintentional channel. This can take the form of key/data-dependent timing variations, power supply fluctuations or electromagnetic emissions. Analysis techniques are well known (see [12] [13]) and can be very powerful against unprotected implementations, including best-practice algorithm designs such as AES. Fortunately, modern smart cards are well protected against such attacks, with a range of countermeasures that mainly impede statistical averaging of signals (used to detect signals in noise) or reduce the source generation of the leakage. Attack countermeasures include:

- Power smoothing
- Noise insertion
- Randomisation of execution
- Timing equalisation
- Dual-rail logic (or Dual CPUs)

The SLE78 chip used in the MULTOS card has a sophisticated dual processing arrangement known as "Integrity Guard" that is believed to be effective at suppressing leakage at source, and this coupled with the Common Criteria certified MULTOS secured OS would suggest that no significant further performance degradation would be incurred from application level countermeasures.

The S3CC9E8 used in the native implementation is a traditional secured microcontroller chip with a single CPU and so it will include some noise smoothing and execution randomisation, but will not suppress the leakage signals at source. Given the age of the chip one would expect some extra side-channel leakage protection to be required from the software, which will have a performance impact. Our tests already included a dummy XOR to represent masking the data used in the crypto-coprocessor, however for this type of chip more help would be needed. One technique used for fast, but perhaps "leaky" crypro-processors is to run the algorithm multiple times, so that an attacker does not know which run used the correct data rather than a dummy pattern. Clearly if you hide your data in a 10 algorithm sequence, you would expect to lose an order of magnitude in performance. Hamming weight equalisation is another technique (used in non-secured CPUs) that seeks to reduce information leakage by ensuring that for each bit transition there is a complementary transition; so as a '1' changes to '0' there is also a '0' changing to '1'. In principle this should reduce leakage, however due to electrical, timing and physical layout factors, register bits do not contribute equally to leakage, so the reduction is inferior to hardware measures and may not justify the effort. In a practical implementation this could for example be a 16-bit processor where the lower 8-bits of a register handle the normal data and the upper 8-bits handle the complementary data. This alone is not sufficient as it is necessary to also clear the registers before and after use and so rather than a two-fold reduction in performance, at least an order of magnitude should be anticipated.

D. Observations

It is likely that physical and fault attack protection can be handled by the smart card hardware without significantly degrading performance. For the MULTOS card based on the SLE78 we have sophisticated hardware coupled to an OS designed for the highest levels of security, and Common Criteria evaluation checks for strong protection against side-channel leakage. For the native implementation in the S3CC9E8 we

TABLE VIII. CARD INTERFACE TRANSMISSION TIMES (ms)

Bytes	Contact (bits/s)			Contactless (bits/s)	
	13441	78125	312500	106000	424000
8	4.76	0.82	0.20	0.60	0.15
16	9.52	1.64	0.41	1.21	0.30
20	11.90	2.05	0.51	1.51	0.38
32	19.05	3.28	0.82	2.42	0.60
40	23.81	4.10	1.02	3.02	0.75
64	28.09	6.55	1.64	4.83	1.21
128	76.19	13.11	3.28	9.66	2.42
192	114.28	19.66	4.92	14.49	3.62

would anticipate additional side-channel countermeasures in software and if we consider the techniques in the earlier section then losing an order of magnitude in performance should be expected.

The motivation for a side-channel attack just to capture the EMV session keys is questionable, however discovery of the keys might expose other assets or assist with sophisticated attack strategies. Therefore, it would be prudent to consider an order of magnitude speed degradation when considering the results in Table VII; although processing would still be fast, with the worst case time for a 192 byte payload being just over 21ms for the slowest mode. However, to know whether this processing is fast enough, or the bottleneck for the protocol, we need to also consider the communication speed via the smart card to Point of Sale (POS) interface.

VII. Communication Effects on Performance

Performance tests of AE, normally just focus on the processing aspects, as communication in an Internet-connected world is generally fast enough (e.g., 25-100Mbps) to cause negligible delay. However, for payment card use of AE we are dealing with interfaces that may be *much* slower and so transactions might hit communication limits before card processing limits.

A. Payment Card Interfaces

The interfaces for payment cards fall into two main categories. The contact interface is the oldest and has dominated payment card transactions using Chip & PIN, however many cards now support the contactless interface for touch and pay (no PIN). Within the standards (contact [8] and contactless [9]) a range of interface speeds are defined, however this does not mean the fastest modes are supported in all deployed cards, or POS terminals. Table VIII shows an example range of transmission speeds and an estimation of the time to transmit the data associated with the different sized test messages. Note that the working interface speed is negotiated and agreed between the smart card and the POS terminal as part of the pre-transaction protocol and by varying clock speed as well as divider parameters the full range would be closer to 9600 - 38400 bits/s. For example the contact rates in Table VIII are computed in accordance with standards, as a clock frequency (5 MHz) f_c divided by factor D (372, 512 and 512 respectively) and multiplied by a factor F (1, 8 and 32 respectively).

The speed range is very wide especially in the contact case, as the default rates maintain compatibility with very old cards and POS terminals. The command processing and transmission can be considered as separate activities; and whichever takes longer is considered the bottleneck limit. Recalling the MULTOS platform performance (Table III) we have a processing limited solution. There are some message/mode combinations that are communications limited, but only when running at the lowest default speed, which is impractically slow. If we now recall the raw native mode results (Table VII), then in practice we have a communications limited solution. At the fastest interface speeds this may not be quite the case, however we would not normally assume that the fastest rates would be available from cards and POS terminals; and so the 78,125 bps and 106,000 bps for contact and contactless interfaces respectively would be more reasonable expectations. The future outlook is that the communication rates will get faster and the contact interface will eventually be displaced by contactless, which suggests that transactions will be processing limited. EMV implementations in mobile phones will of course have access to much faster wireless technologies such as 802.11ac that can run at 1.3 Gbits/s, however the scope of this study is restricted to conventional smart card devices.

VIII. Conclusions

The study investigated AE modes on existing available smart chips/platforms using conventional crypto-coprocessors. GCM was not analysed in detail as the *multH* function (or parts of it) would need to be implemented within more specialist crypto-coprocessor hardware. All the other AE modes considered, were feasible both in terms of speed and memory usage. The native mode implementation was much faster than the MULTOS platform and in the final tests all the modes for all single APDU test message sizes took no more than 2.14ms.

The new results differ markedly from previous comparisons that have focussed on general processors, larger message sizes and the inclusion of Associated Data. The native ETM/CCM modes were quicker than OCB for the single APDU test messages although OCB modes would be expected to claw back the advantage for multi-APDU messages. In our native implementation, and for a single APDU, ETM was always slightly ahead of CCM and OCB2 led OCB3.

At first glance the results may seem counter-intuitive due to the extra encryptions required in ETM/CCM compared to OCB2/OCB3, however they arise because the chip has significant crypto-coprocessor gain. The native measurements show that the core DES encryption time is comparable with a 16 byte block XOR executed by the CPU. We suggested a new benchmark, the Technology Independent Gain Assessment (TIGA) for CPUs with crypto-coprocessors; as the percentage of the block encryption that can be completed by the crypto-coprocessor in the time it would take the CPU to compute a block XOR. We estimated that the MULTOS platform and native chip had TIGAs of 22% and 100% (33% for TDES) respectively. The new TIGA measure could be valuable when comparing algorithm implementations on various platform types, as may increasingly be the case in Internet of Things implementations.

The performance gain from the crypto-coprocessor can be eroded if more time is spent conditioning the data into and out of it. Such processing may be required for security protection, (to mask data and/or to reduce leakage), although it should be noted that any part of an algorithm running in the CPU may also require similar protection.

The processing time comparison was independent of the communications interface speed, however both affect the overall protocol performance. The MULTOS platform is primarily processing limited, whereas the simple native implementation is mainly communications limited. If we degrade the native performance by an order of magnitude in anticipation of overheads to reduce side-channel leakage (e.g., repeated operations or hamming weight equalisation in software) then we approach the optimum around the 78,125bps rate; any lower than this and the protocol performance will degrade due to communication delays.

The crypto-coprocessor gain, coupled with small message sizes, means that there is not much to choose between OCB2, OCB3, ETM and CCM performance. It might be argued that ETM could be chosen for speed and efficiency of small-/medium messages or OCB if medium/large messages are the norm. It is also possible for GCM to be usable in future if supported by a specialist co-processor, however it is unlikely to be much quicker than the other modes. As performance is unlikely to be a great differentiator for the AE modes, an option could be to standardise an AE framework around a default mode and define a negotiation process for a card and POS terminal to agree alternative AE modes. This would provide a useful mechanism if vulnerabilities were discovered in any particular AE mode, as well as a means for interworking and migration of smart cards and POS terminals having different capabilities.

A. Future Work

It would be interesting to implement the AE modes in a similar manner on other secured microcontrollers with crypto-coprocessors (although this may be difficult due to publication restrictions required by device vendors). In the first instance this should help prove the generality of the results, but also provide more evidence on the usefulness of the TIGA benchmark, which is easily determined on any processor. It is hoped that a secured smart card microcontroller chip could become available (for academic research) offering native mode programming and crypto-coprocessor support for GCM, so that a full-set of AE mode results could be generated and published. A Java Card platform has become available that would permit direct comparison with the MULTOS platform, as both are based on the SLE78 secured microcontroller.

REFERENCES

[1] D. Boneh, R. Demillo, and R. Lipton, "On the importance of checking computations", in *Advances in Cryptography - Eurocrypt 97*, volume 1233, pp. 37-51, Springer Verlag, 2013.

[2] CC, "Common criteria for information technology security evaluation part1: Introduction and general model," version 3.1 release 4, September 2012.

[3] EMV, "Books 1-4," Version 4.3, 2011.

[4] EMVCo, http://www.emvco.com/ [retrieved: March, 2017].

[5] FIPS, "Federal information Processing Standards, Data Encryption Standard (DES), publication 46-3" http://csrc.nist.gov/publications/fips/fips46-3/fips46-3.pdf [retrieved: March, 2017].

[6] FIPS, "Federal Information Processing Standards, Announcing the Advanced Encryption Standard (AES), Publication 197." http://nvlpubs.nist.gov/nistpubs/FIPS/NIST.FIPS.197.pdf [retrieved: March, 2017].

[7] Infineon, "SLE78CAFX4000P(M) short product overview," v11.12, 2012.

[8] ISO/IEC, "7816 identification cards - integrated circuit(s) cards with contacts," parts 1-4, 1999.

[9] ISO/IEC, "14443 identification cards - contactless integrated circuit cards - proximity cards," parts 1-4, 2008.

[10] ISO/IEC, "19772 Information technology - Security techniques - Authenticated encryption," 2009.

[11] ISO/IEC, "9797 Information technology - Security techniques - Message Authentication Codes (MACs)," parts 1-3, 2011.

[12] P. Kocher, "Timing attacks on implementations of diffie-hellman RSA DSS and other systems," in *Advances in Cryptology - CRYPTO '96 Proceedings LNCS*, volume 1109, pp. 104-113 Springer Verlag, 1996.

[13] P. Kocher, J. Jaffe, and B. Jun, "Differential power analysis," in *Advances in Cryptology - Crypto 99 Proceedings LNCS*, volume 1666, pp. 388-397, Springer Verlag, 1999.

[14] T. Krovetz and P. Rogaway, "The software performance of authenticated encryption modes, fast software encryption, RFC 7253," in *FSE 2011 Proceedings*, pp. 306-327, Springer verlag, 2011.

[15] T. Krovetz and P. Rogaway, "The OCB authenticated-encryption algorithm, IETF RFC 7253," May 2014.

[16] D. McGrew and J. Viega, "The galois/counter mode of operation (GCM)," parts 1-3, May 2005, http://csrc.nist.gov/groups/ST/toolkit/BCM/documents/proposedmodes/gcm/gcm-spec.pdf [retrieved: March, 2017].

[17] MULTOS, http://www.multos.com/ [retrieved: March, 2017].

[18] MULTOS, "The MULTOS developer's reference manual," MAO-DOC-TEC-006 v1.49, 2013.

[19] NIST, "Recommendation for block cipher modes of operation: The CCM mode for authentication and confidentiality, SP800-38C," May 2004.

[20] NIST, "Recommendation for block cipher modes of operation: Galois/-counter mode (GCM) and GMAC, SP800-38D," November 2007.

[21] P. Rogaway, "OCB mode," http://web.cs.ucdavis.edu/~rogaway/ocb/ [retrieved: March, 2017].

[22] J. Salowey, A. Choudhury, and D. McGrew, "AES galois counter mode (GCM) cipher suites for TLS, IETF RFC 5288," August 2008.

[23] Samsung, "S3CC9E4/8: 16-bit CMOS microcontroller for smart card user's manual," rev 0, 2004.

[24] D. Whiting, R. Housley, and N. Ferguson, "Counter with CBC-MAC (CCM), IETF RFC 3610," September 2003.

Distributed System Behavior Modeling of Urban Systems with Ontologies, Rules and Many-to-Many Association Relationships

Maria Coelho and Mark A. Austin
Department of Civil and Environmental Engineering,
University of Maryland, College Park, MD 20742, USA
E-mail: memc30@hotmail.com; austin@isr.umd.edu

Mark Blackburn
Stevens Institute of Technology,
Hoboken, NJ 07030, USA
E-mail: mblackbu@stevens.edu

***Abstract*—Modern societal-scale infrastructures are defined by spatially distributed network structures, concurrent subsystem-level behaviors, distributed control and decision making, and interdependencies among subsystems that are not always well understood. This work-in-progress paper presents a model of system-level interactions that simulates distributed system behaviors through the use of ontologies, rules checking, message passing mechanisms, and mediators. We take initial steps toward the behavior modeling of large-scale urban networks as collections of networks that interact via many-to-many association relationships. The preliminary implementation is a collection of families interacting with a collection of school systems. We conclude with ideas for scaling up the simulations with mediators assembled from Apache Camel technology.**

Keywords-Systems Engineering; Ontologies; Behavior Modeling; Mediator; Network Communication.

I. INTRODUCTION

A. Problem Statement

The modern way of life is enabled by remarkable advances in technology (e.g., the Internet, smart mobile devices, cloud computing) and the development of urban systems (e.g., transportation, electric power, wastewater facilities and water supply networks, among others) whose operations and interactions have superior levels of performance, extended functionality and good economics. While end-users applaud the benefits that these technological advances afford, model-based systems engineers are faced with a multitude of new design challenges that can be traced to the presence of heterogeneous content (multiple disciplines), network structures that are spatial, multi-layer, interwoven and dynamic, and behaviors that are distributed and concurrent. As a case in point, modern urban infrastructure systems comprise physical, communication and social networks that are spatially distributed, and defined by concurrent subsystem-level behaviors, distributed control and decision making, and interdependencies among subsystems that are not always well understood. In the past, engineers have kept these difficulties in check by designing subsystems that operate as independently as possible from one another. Today, however, it is recognized that subsystem independence and inferior levels of situational awareness come at a cost of sub-optimal functionality and performance. Overcoming these barriers makes future challenges in urban systems design and management are a lot more difficult than they used to be.

B. Cascading Failures in Decentralized Systems

In a decentralized system structure, no decision maker knows all of the information known to all of the other decision makers, yet as a group, they must cooperate to achieve system-wide objectives. Communication and information exchange are important to the decision makers because communication establishes common knowledge among the decision makers which, in turn, enhances the ability of decision makers to make decisions appropriate to their understanding, or situational awareness, of the system state, its goals and objectives. While each of the participating disciplines may have a preference toward operating their domain as independently as possible from the other disciplines, achieving target levels of performance and correctness of functionality nearly always requires that disciplines coordinate activities at key points in the system operation. And even if the resulting cross-domain relationships are only weakly linked, they are nonetheless, still linked. When part of a system fails, there exists a possibility that the failure will cascade across interdisciplinary boundaries to other correlative infrastructures, and sometimes even back to the originated source, thus making highly connected systems more fragile to various kinds of disturbances than their independent counterparts.

Experience over the past decade with major infrastructure disruptions, such as the 2011 San Diego blackout, the 2003 Northeast blackout, and Hurricane Irene in 2011, has shown that the greatest losses from disruptive events may be distant from where damages started. In another example, Hurricane Katrina disrupted oil terminal operations in southern Louisiana, not because of direct damage to port facilities, but because workers could not reach work locations through surface transportation routes and could not be housed locally because of disruption to potable water supplies, housing, and food shipments [1]. To complicate matters, until very recently infrastructure management systems did not allow a manager of one system to access the operations and conditions of another system. Therefore, emergency managers would fail to recognize this interdependence of infrastructures in responding to an incident, a fact recognized by The National Strategy for the Physical Protection of Critical Infrastructures and Key Assets [2]. In such situations, where there is no information exchange between interdependent systems, interdependencies can lead to cascading disruptions throughout the entire system in unexpected, undesirable and costly ways. The objectives of

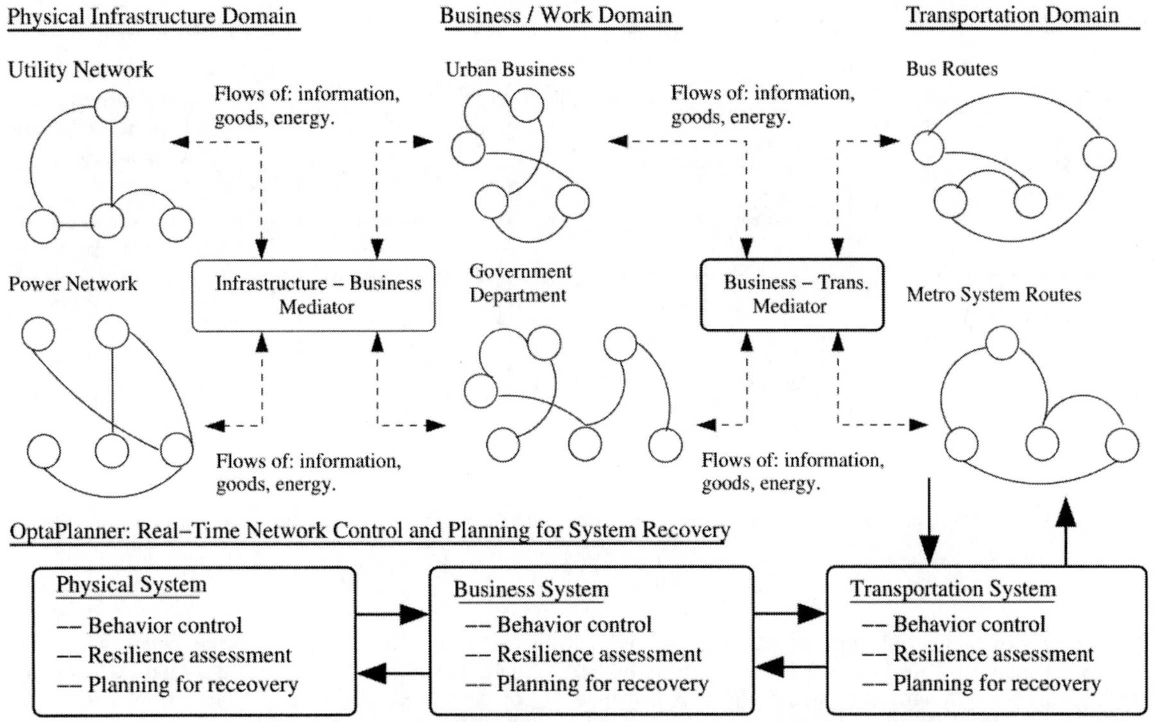

Figure 1. Architecture for multi-domain behavior modeling with many-to-many associations.

this work-in-progress paper are to explore opportunities for overcoming these limitations.

C. Scope and Objectives

In order to understand how cascading failures might be best managed, it is necessary to have the ability to model information exchange at the interdependency boundaries, and to model their consequent effect within a subsystems boundary. This points to a strong need for new capability in modeling and simulation of urban infrastructure systems as system-of-systems, and the explicit capture of infrastructure interdependencies. We envision such a system having an architecture along the lines shown in Figure 1, and eventually, tools such as OptaPlanner [3] providing strategies for real-time control of behaviors, assessment of domain resilience and planning of recover actions in response to severe events. Instead of modeling the dynamic behavior of systems with centralized control and one large catch-all ontology, our work explores opportunities for modeling systems as collections of discipline-specific (or community) networks that will dynamically evolve in response to events. Each community will have a graph that evolves according to a set of community-specific rules, and subject to satisfaction of constraints. Communities will interact when then need to in order to achieve system-level objectives. If goals are in conflict, or resources are insufficient, then negotiation will need to take place.

This work-in-progress paper presents a model of system-level interactions that simulates distributed system behaviors through the use of ontologies, rules checking, and message passing mechanisms. The architecture builds upon the framework presented by Austin et al. [4], and in particular, extends the distributed behavior modeling capability from one-to-one association relationships among communities to many-to-many association relationships among networked communities.

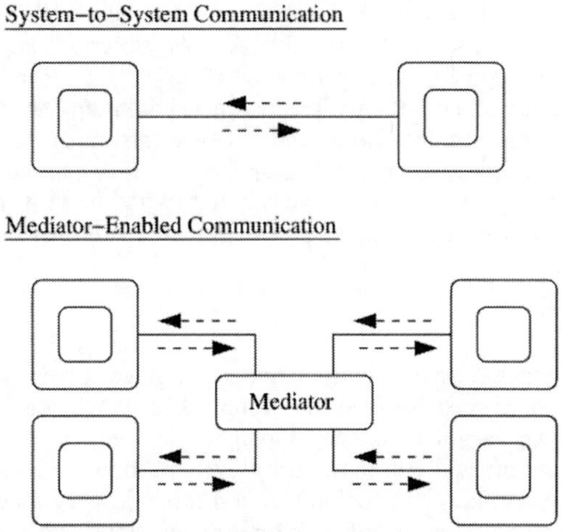

Figure 2. Framework for communication among systems of type A and B.

As illustrated in Figure 2, one-to-one association relationships can be modeled with exchange of messages in a point-to-point communication setup. The top part of the figure shows point-to-point communication in a one-to-one association relationship between systems. Mediator enabled communication in a many-to-many association relationship among systems are shown in the bottom half of the figure.

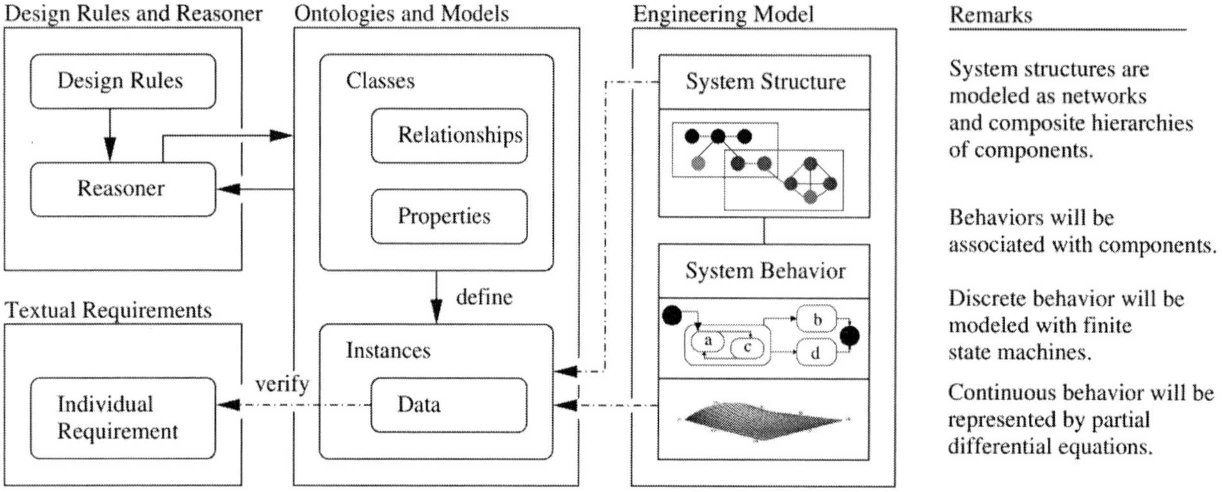

Figure 3. Framework for implementation of semantic models using ontologies, rules, and reasoning mechanisms (Adapted from Delgoshaei, Austin and Nguyen [5]).

Many-to-many association relationship among systems are enabled by collections of mediators. Each ontology is paired with an interface for communication and information exchange with other ontologies. From a communications standpoint, this architectural setup is simpler than what is commonly found in multi-hop routing of messages in wireless sensor networks.

Section II covers the relationship of ontologies and rules to our related work in model-based systems engineering, Section III describes several aspects of our work in progress, including: (1) Distributed system behavior modeling with ontologies and rules, and (2) Use of mediators for behavior modeling of distributed systems having many-to-many association relationships among connected networks. We describe the software architecture for an experimental platform for assembling ensembles of community graphs and simulating their discrete, event-based interactions, and exercise this capability with an application involving collections of families interacting with multiple school systems. We conclude with ideas for scaling up the simulations with mediators assembled from Apache Camel technology.

II. Related Work

Model-based systems engineering development is an approach to systems-level development in which the focus and primary artifacts of development are models, as opposed to documents. As engineering systems become increasingly complex the need for automation arises [6]. A tenet of our work is that methodologies for strategic approaches to design will employ semantic descriptions of application domains, and use ontologies and rule-based reasoning to enable validation of requirements, automated synthesis of potentially good design solutions, and communication (or mappings) among multiple disciplines [7] [8] [9].

Figure 3 pulls together the different pieces of the proposed architecture, for distributed system behavior modeling with ontologies, rules, mediators and message passing mechanisms. On the left-hand side, the textual requirements are defined in terms of mathematical and logical rule expressions for design rule checking. Engineering models will correspond to a multitude of graph structure and composite hierarchy structures for the system structure and system behavior. Behaviors will be associated with components. Discrete behavior will be modeled with finite state machines. Continuous behaviors will be represented as the solution to ordinary and partial differential equations. Ontology models and rules will glue the requirements to the engineering models and provide a platform for simulating the development of system structures, adjustments to system structure over time, and system behavior. This is a work in progress [10] [5].

III. Work in Progress

Topic 1. Distributed System Behavior Modeling with Ontologies and Rules

Figure 4 shows the software architecture for distributed system behavior modeling for collections of graphs that have dynamic behavior defined by ontology classes, relationships among ontology classes, ontology and data properties, listeners, mediators and message passing mechanisms. The abstract ontology model class contains concepts common to all ontologies (e.g., the ability to receive message input). Domain-specific ontologies are extensions of the abstract ontology classes. They add a name space and build the ontology classes, relationships among classes, properties of classes for the domain. Instances (see Figure 3) are semantic objects in the domain.

By themselves, the ontologies provide a framework for the representation of knowledge, but otherwise, cannot do much and really arent that interesting. This situation changes when domain-specific rules are imported into the model and graph transformations are enabled by formal reasoning and event-based input from external sources. Distributed behavior modeling involves multiple semantic models, multiple sets of rules, mechanisms of communication among semantic models, and data input, possibly from multiple sources. We provide this functionality in our distributed behavior model by loosely coupling each semantic model to a semantic interface. Each

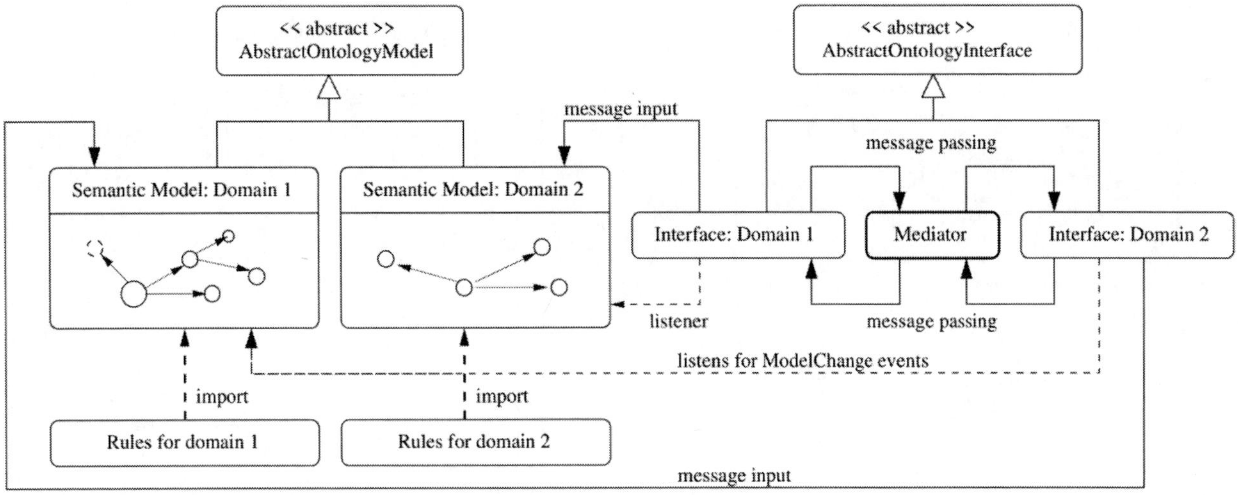

Figure 4. System architecture for distributed system behavior modeling with ontologies, rules, mediators and message passing mechanisms.

semantic interface listens for changes to the semantic domain graph and when required, forwards the essential details of the change to other domains (interfaces) that have registered interest in receiving notification of such changes. They also listen for incoming messages from external semantic models. Since changes to the graph structure are triggered by events (e.g., the addition of an individual; an update to a data property value; a new association relationship among objects), a central challenge is design of the rules and ontology structure so that the interfaces will always be notified when exchanges of data and information need to occur. Individual messages are defined by their type (e.g., MessageType.miscellaneous), a message source and destination, and a reference to the value of the data being exchanged. The receiving interface will forward incoming messages to the semantic model, which, in turn, may trigger an update to the graph model. Since end-points of the basic message passing infrastructure are common to all semantic model interfaces, it makes sense to define it in an abstract ontology interface model.

Topic 2. Mediator Design

When the number of participating applications domains is very small, point-to-point channel communication between interfaces is practical. Otherwise, an efficient way of handling domain communication is by delegating the task of sending and receiving specific requests to a central object. In software engineering, a common pattern used to solve this problem is the Mediator Pattern.

As illustrated in Figures 1 and 2, the mediator pattern defines a object responsible for the overall communication of the system, which from here on out will be referred as the mediator object. The mediator has the role of a router, it centralizes the logic to send and receive messages. Components of the system send messages to the mediator rather than to the other components; likewise, they rely on the mediator to send change notifications to them [11]. The implementation of this pattern greatly simplifies the other classes in the system; components are more generic since they no longer have to contain logic to manage communication with other components. Because other components remain generic, the mediator has to be application specific in order to encapsulate application-specific behavior. One can reuse all other classes for other applications, and only need to rewrite the mediator class for the new application.

Topic 3. Apache Camel

Looking to the future, we envision a full-scale implementation of distributed behavior modeling (see Figure 1) having to transmit a multiplicity of message types and content, with the underlying logic needed to deliver messages possibly being a lot more complicated than send message A in domain B to domain C. Our present-day capability is simplified in the sense that domain interfaces are assumed to be homogeneous. But looking forward, this will not always be true. This situation points to a strong need for new approaches to the construction and operation of message passing mechanisms.

One promising approach that we will explore is Apache Camel [12] [13], an open source Java framework that focuses on making Enterprise Integration Patterns (EIP) accessible through carefully designed interfaces, base objects, commonly needed implementations, debugging tools and a configuration system. Figure 5 shows, for example, a platform infrastructure for behavior modeling of three connected application (networked) domains. In addition to basic content-based routing, Apache Camel provides support for filtering and transformation of messages.

IV. Case Study Problem

To illustrate the capabilities of our experimental architecture, we now present the essential details of a simulation framework for the behavior modeling of a multiplicity of families and school, defined by ontologies, rules, and exchange of information as messages. Figure 6 is an instantiation of the concepts introduced in Figure 4 and shows the software architecture for a family-school interaction. And Figure 7 is the network setup for three families interacting with elementary, middle and high schools.

As every parent knows, the enrollment process involves the exchange of specific information, such as the name, birth

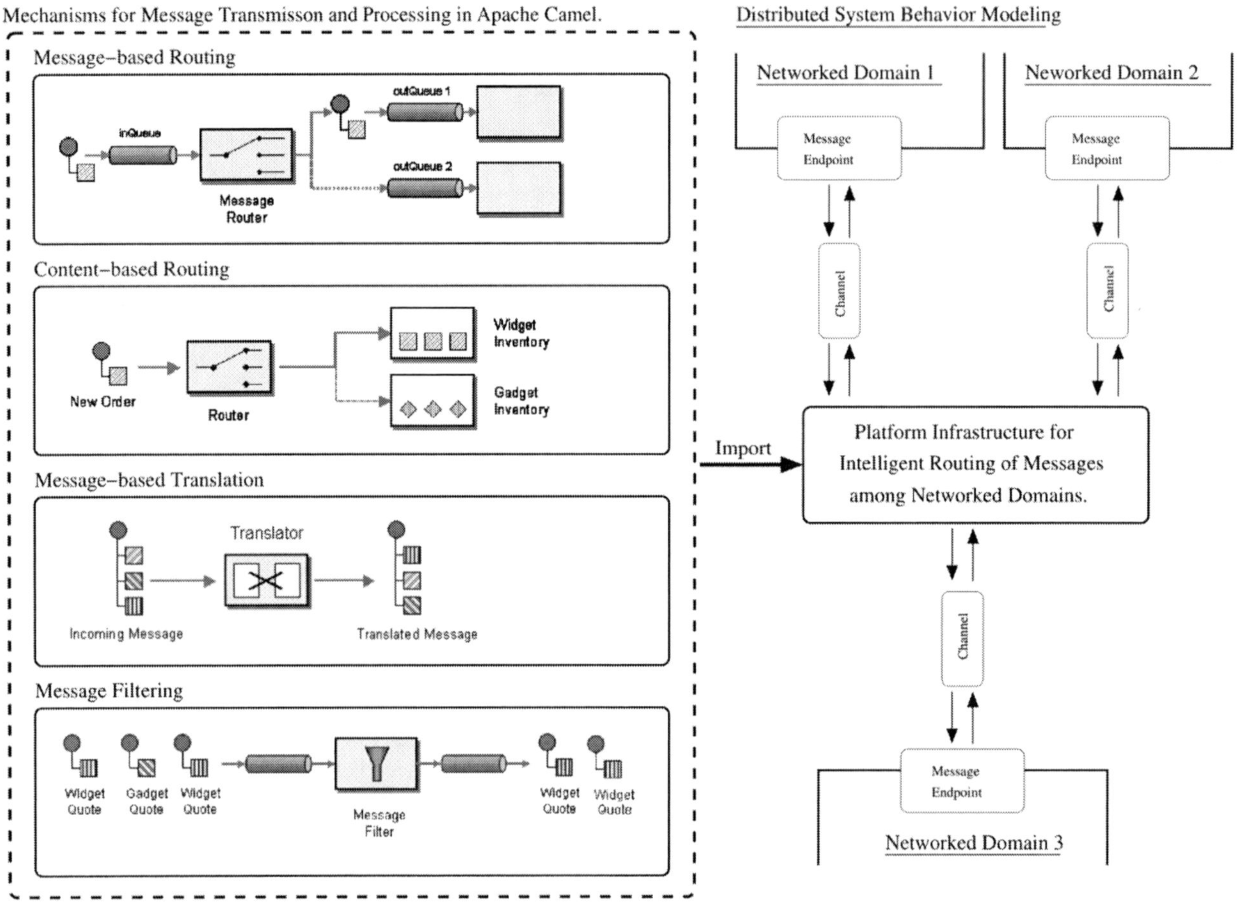

Figure 5. Platform infrastructure for distributed behavior modeling and intelligent communication (message passing) among networked domains.

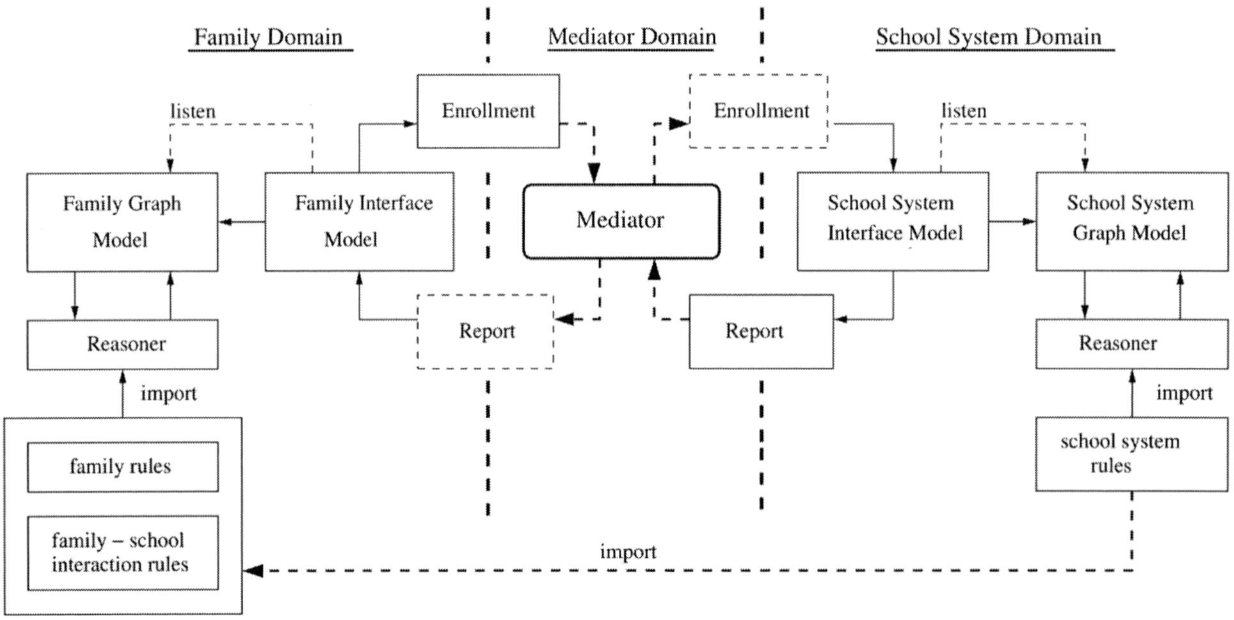

Figure 6. Software architecture for distributed behavior modeling in the family-school case study.

date, home address and social security number of each child. Then, once the child is accepted the school system takes over. They figure out what grade level is appropriate for each child, what classroom the child will be in, the schedule of learning activities, and when school reports will be sent home.

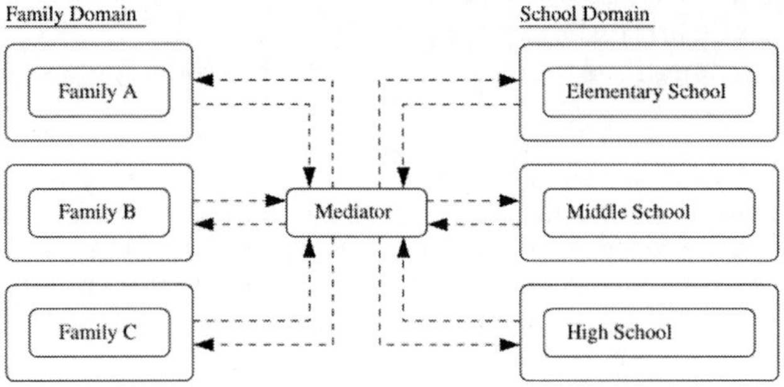

Figure 7. Framework for communication among multiple families and schools enabled by a mediator.

Communication among the family and school communities is handled by a mediator. Every component of the system (i.e., families and schools) register with the mediator as listeners. Once a family member reaches a certain age, the age rules associated with the family system will trigger a school enrollment form to be sent to the mediator in the form of a message, with source and destination properties. The mediator logic loops through all of its registered listeners to find a match with the message destination, and then destination listener is notified. Similarly, once the system calendar reaches a certain date, the reporting rules associated with the school system will trigger a school report to be sent to the mediator. The messaging design allows the school enrollment form to be received only by the school of interest, and not broadcasted to the entire school system. Likewise, this design allows the school reports to be sent only to the students family. This mediator logic design is known as point-to-point channel, and it ensures that only one listener consumes any given message. The channel can have multiple listeners that consume multiple messages concurrently, but the design ensures that only one of them can successfully consume a particular message. Using this approach, listeners do not have to coordinate with each other; coordination could be complex, create a lot of communication overhead, and increase coupling between otherwise independent receivers.

V. Conclusions and Future Work

This paper has focused on the design and preliminary implementation of a message passing infrastructure needed to support communication in many-to-many association relationships connecting domain-specific networks.

Our long-term research objective is computational support for the design, simulation, and validation of models of distributed behavior in real-world urban environments. The family-school distributed behavior model is merely a starting point. We anticipate that the end-result will look something like Figure 1, and provide strategies for real-time control of behaviors, assessment of domain resilience, and planning of recovery actions in response to severe events. Models of urban data and system state will be coupled to tools for spatial and temporal reasoning, and will synchronize with layers of domain-specific visualization (not shown in Figure 1). In order to drive the design and validation of domain rules, and rules for exchange of messages between domains, we will design and simulate a series of progressively complicated urban case study problems.

Our future work will investigate opportunities for using Apache Camel technology in this context, especially as problem sizes and the number of participating domains scale up. A second important topic for future work is linkage of our simulation framework to tools for optimization and tradeoff analysis. Such tools would allow decision makers to examine the sensitivity of design outcomes to parameter choices, understand the impact of resource constraints, understand system stability in the presence of fluctuations to modeling parameter values, and potentially, even understand emergent interactions among systems.

References

[1] C. A. Myers, T. Slack, and J. Singelmann, "Social Vulnerability and Migration in the Wake of Disaster: The case of Hurricanes Katrina and Rita," Population and Environment, vol. 29, 2008, pp. 271–291.

[2] White House (2003), The National Strategy for the Physical Protection of Critical Infrastructures and Key Assets. Washington, DC.

[3] OptaPlanner (2016), A Constraint-Satisfaction Solver. For details, see: https://www.optaplanner.org (Accessed, Jan 4., 2017).

[4] M. A. Austin, P. Delgoshaei, and A. Nguyen, "Distributed Systems Behavior Modeling with Ontologies, Rules, and Message Passing Mechanisms," in Thirteenth Annual Conference on Systems Engineering Research (CSER 2015), Hoboken, New Jersey, March 17-19 2015, pp. 373–382.

[5] P. Delgoshaei, M. A. Austin, and A. Pertzborn, "*A Semantic Framework for Modeling and Simulation of Cyber-Physical Systems*," in International Journal On Advances in Systems and Measurements, Vol. 7, No. 3-4, December, 2014, pp. 223–238., 2014.

[6] M. A. Austin and J. S. Baras, An Introduction to Information-Centric Systems Engineering. Toulouse, France: Tutorial F06, INCOSE, June 2004.

[7] M. A. Austin, V. Mayank, and N. Shmunis, "Ontology-Based Validation of Connectivity Relationships in a Home Theater System," 21st International Journal of Intelligent Systems, vol. 21, no. 10, October 2006, pp. 1111–1125.

[8] ——, "PaladinRM: Graph-Based Visualization of Requirements Organized for Team-Based Design," Systems Engineering: The Journal of the International Council on Systems Engineering, vol. 9, no. 2, May 2006, pp. 129–145.

[9] N. Nassar and M. A. Austin, "Model-Based Systems Engineering Design and Trade-Off Analysis with RDF Graphs," in 11th Annual Conference on Systems Engineering Research (CSER 2013), Georgia Institute of Technology, Atlanta, GA, March 19-22 2013, pp. 216–225.

[10] P. Delgoshaei, M. A. Austin, and D. A. Veronica, "A Semantic Platform Infrastructure for Requirements Traceability and System Assessment," The Ninth International Conference on Systems (ICONS 2014), February 2014, pp. 215–219.

[11] S. Stelting and O. Maassen, Applied Java Patterns. SUN Microsystems Press, Prentice-Hall, 2002.

[12] C. Ibsen, J. Antsey, and Z. Hadrian, Camel in Action. Manning Publications Company, 2010.

[13] G. Hohpe and B. Woolf, Enterprise Integration Patterns: Designing, Building and Deploying Message Passing Solutions. Addison Wesley, 2004.

Challenges in Functional Testing on the Way to Automated Driving

Steffen Wittel*, Daniel Ulmer* and Oliver Bühler*
*Steinbeis Interagierende Systeme GmbH, Esslingen, Germany
Email: {steffen.wittel,daniel.ulmer,oliver.buehler}@interagierende-systeme.de

***Abstract*—The transition to automated driving poses a major challenge for the automotive industry in the field of functional testing. In current vehicles, the automobile manufacturers are not yet taking full responsibility for the driving maneuvers automatically performed by the vehicles. This will change with automated driving, which means the temporary or complete loss of the human driver as a fallback level in traffic situations that cannot be handled by the vehicle software. During the automated driving, the automobile manufacturers have the responsibility for the vehicle behavior until the handover of the vehicle control to the human driver. The handover requires a reasonable warning period in which the automated driving is to be maintained. Depending on the distraction, the human driver needs some time to perceive the traffic situation and to react appropriately. The warning period will grow due to the increasing automation of driving tasks, which allows the human driver to focus her or his attention on non-driving activities and no longer on a permanent monitoring for an immediate intervention in case of a system malfunction. Extensive testing activities are therefore required to verify the functionality and the safety of the vehicles. This paper presents a systematic approach for the functional testing of automated driving. Especially, the spectrum of possible traffic situations, which the vehicles might be getting into, and the test process have been taken into account by the approach.**

Keywords–Automated Driving; Automotive Testing; Functional Testing; Test Process.

I. Introduction

As published in [2], about 94 % of the road accidents are caused by the human driver due to carelessness, wrong decisions or incorrect performing of driving maneuvers. The human driver is therefore the main cause of the majority of all road accidents and thus offers the greatest potential to improve the traffic safety. Thereby, the driving automation can contribute to the traffic safety by relieving the human driver or taking over partial or complete driving tasks for the longitudinal and lateral control of the vehicle in as many driving scenarios as possible.

The term "automated driving" or "autonomous driving" is used in many different meanings. Several institutions, e.g., the Germany Federal Highway Research Institute (BASt), the US National Highway Traffic Safety Administration (NHTSA), the Society of Automotive Engineers (SAE), as well as the German Association of the Automotive Industry (VDA), have classified the different levels of driving automation. In this paper, the driving automation levels according to SAE J3016 [1] are used:

No Automation: The system does not take over the vehicle control with the exception of short-term interventions of emergency functions in critical traffic situations. The human driver is fully responsible for the vehicle.

Driver Assistance: The vehicle is controlled either in the lateral or longitudinal direction by the system. The human driver controls the remaining direction, while she or he has to monitor the behavior of the vehicle and has to intervene immediately in case of a critical situation.

Partial Automation: The system controls the longitudinal and lateral direction. The human driver has to monitor the behavior of the vehicle and has to intervene immediately in case of a critical situation.

Conditional Automation: The vehicle control is done in the longitudinal and lateral direction by the system. The human driver has to react within a reasonable time after a warning by the system.

High Automation: The system controls the longitudinal and lateral direction, and has to handle all traffic situations, even if the human driver does not react appropriately.

Full Automation: The system has to handle all traffic situations.

With the increasing automation of the driving tasks, the automobile manufacturers are taking over more and more responsibility from the human driver and thus for the driving maneuvers automatically performed by the vehicles as shown in Table I. While the first safety assistance systems, like the Electronic Stability Control (ESC) [3] or the Antilock Braking System (ABS) [3], only supported the driver to cope with critical situations, the advanced driver assistance systems that are nowadays on the market additionally provide comfort functions for specific driving scenarios. But until now, the automotive manufacturers were able to use the human driver as a fallback level in a case where the system could not handle the situation. With each step in the direction towards automated

TABLE I. Overview about the driving automation levels based on SAE J3016 [1].

Name	*Functions*	*Monitoring*	*Controlling*	*Fallback*	*Responsibility*
No Automation	None	Human Driver	Human Driver	Human Driver	Human Driver
Driver Assistance	Some	Human Driver	System / Human Driver	Human Driver	Human Driver
Partial Automation	Some	Human Driver	System	Human Driver	Human Driver
Conditional Automation	Some	System	System	Human Driver	Automobile Manufacturer / Human Driver
High Automation	Some	System	System	System	Automobile Manufacturer
Full Automation	All	System	System	System	Automobile Manufacturer

driving, the operating hours, as well as the time until the takeover of the vehicle control, is increased and in consequence the period of time for which the automotive manufacturers are responsible for the vehicle.

Current testing activities do not adequately take into account the large number of different environmental conditions and timing behaviors, which occur in the real road traffic. They are primarily used to test representative driving scenarios previously selected by test methods. A dynamic variation of the test scenarios is usually performed on rare occasions and if only in narrow limits. But the reality shows that two test drives carried out on different days between the same starting point and destination can have significant differences. They differ in the number of road users and their driving behaviors. Moreover, different weather conditions cause varieties in the information provided by the sensors and the driveability of the road. In both cases, the vehicle has to reach the destination complying with the road traffic regulations without endangering occupants or other road users.

The approach presented in this paper takes into account the spectrum of possible traffic situations the vehicles might be getting into. Therefore, it proposes a prioritization during the test execution by dividing the system behavior into a functional and a temporal part. Moreover, it recommends an optimization of the test process to overcome with the huge number of tests cases expected for the testing of automated driving.

The following section shows the related work. Section III evaluates the weaknesses of human drivers in the road traffic and shows how driving automation can play a part in contributing to traffic safety. Finally, Section IV presents the challenges of the automobile manufacturers to ensure a safe operation of automated driving.

II. Related Work

The national research project with the name "PEGASUS" [4], founded by the Federal Ministry for Economic Affairs and Energy (BMWi) in conjunction with automotive companies, suppliers, small and medium-sized companies and research institutes from Germany, should provide standards for the automated driving to close essential gaps in the field of testing and the release of vehicles. Among others, the research project should answer the questions, which requirements must meet self-driving vehicles, how can the safety and reliability of these systems be demonstrated and what role does the human factor play in the future. As published by the project [4], new and uniform quality standards and methods are necessary for the accreditation of automated driving functions. The project goal is to establish generally accepted quality criteria, tools and methods. Moreover, scenarios and situations shall be provided for the release of automated driving functions, as well as procedures for the testing. The main objectives of the project are:

a) Definition of a common approach in the testing of automated vehicle systems in the simulation, at test benches and in real-world environments
b) Development of a continuous and flexible tool chain for the testing of automated driving
c) Integration of the tests in the development process at an early stage
d) Creation of a test method for automated driving features across manufactures

While so far the complexity and performance of the vehicle were limited by the hardware, the embedded software, as well as the development and test process, now seem to be the limiting factors as elaborate in [5]. The report predicts that the distribution of the functionality over several components leads to a level of testing beyond the economical and temporal feasible possibilities. Thus, the authors see the testing of such systems, which have to work in all possible traffic situations, as one of the highest technical hurdles. The report shows that there is a lack of metrics, which represent the system and allow a comparison between different systems.

According to [6], driving automation can bypass current risks, but can also lead to new risks, which do not exist so far. The paper shows that "demonstrating safety of automated driving in advance of introduction is nearly impossible". Thereby, they illustrate that the necessary number of kilometers to demonstrate the safety of a system cannot be provided economically by real test vehicles due to the complexity of the possible traffic situations. The statement is based, among others, on the assumptions that the number of kilometers cannot be driven in the available time for testing and that the testing must be repeated after changes in the software or hardware.

III. Road Accidents

Over the years, the number of road accidents rose with the increasing number of road users in Germany as shown in Figure 1. But this did not lead to an increase in the number of injured or dead people in road accidents. The technical progress in passive and active safety systems of vehicles significantly contributed to the mitigation of the road accidents

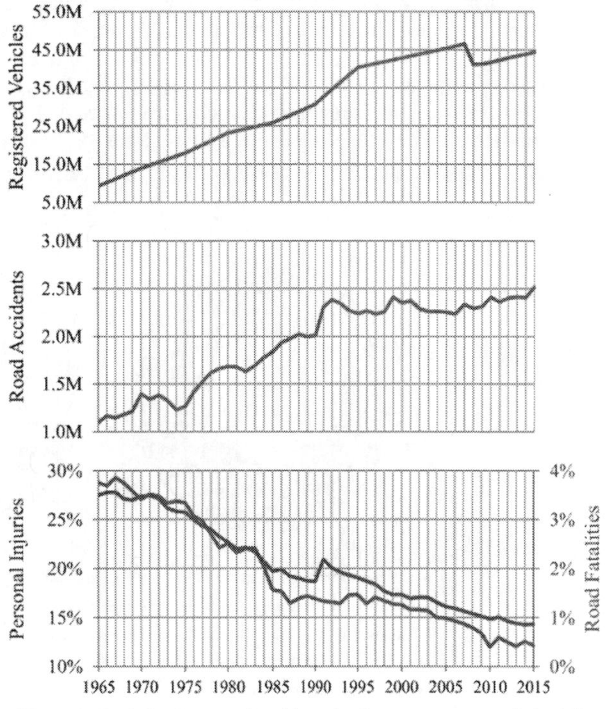

Figure 1. Statistic about road accidents in Germany over a period of 50 years [7].

and personal injuries. Safety systems, which already belong to the standard equipment of almost all new vehicles on the market, prevent road accidents or reduce their impact. Thereby, driving automation helps to eliminate weaknesses of human drivers by finding appropriate reactions in critical situations.

As explained in Section I, the human driver is the main cause of the majority of road accidents. The road accidents statistic [7] shows mistakes of human drivers in Germany, which led to road accidents that were reported to the police. These are mainly the accidents with serious consequences. Minor road accidents with material damages only or minor injuries are not covered by the statistic, because they are usually not reported to the police. A list of common areas in which mistakes made by an improper driving of human drivers can be categorized, is presented in the following as provided by the Federal Statistical Office of Germany:

a) Use of the road
b) Speed
c) Distance
d) Overtaking
e) Driving past
f) Driving side by side
g) Priority, precedence
h) Turning, U-turn, reversing, entering the flow of traffic, starting off the edge of the road
i) Improper behavior towards pedestrians
j) Stationary vehicles, safety measures
k) Failure to observe lighting regulations

The list shows the complexity of road traffic and the potential mistakes of a human driver. In addition to the human driver, other road users are usually in the surroundings and their misbehavior must be taken into account as well. According to [8], driving in a dynamic environment is subject to a variety of cognitive demands of the human driver. The human driver has to correctly perceive relevant objects and events, interpret them, and derive his or her actions from them. It is also necessary to recognize new circumstances and make appropriate adjustments well enough in advance.

When looking at the road accident statistic of Germany as visualized in Figure 2, it is noticeable that the risk potential varies according to the street location. Within villages or towns, road accidents occur due to the accumulation of road users or confusing traffic situations. There are a lot of different reasons for road accidents in urban environments, which can be seen at the large number of road accidents (14.5 %) that could not be assigned to one of the major causes. In non-urban environments, there are first focus areas that are the result of the increased velocity in comparison with urban environments. With more than 30 percent of all road accidents in non-urban environments, leaving the carriageway is the most common reason. On freeways, the human driver is confronted with a simpler road characteristic, which limits the number of causes for road accidents. Almost half of all road accidents on the freeway are rear-end collisions.

The number of road facilities and seriously injured people in urban environments (14.5 %) represent in total a lower percentage than in non-urban environments (25.7 %) or freeways (19.1 %) as illustrated in Figure 3. But the absolute values show that most of the people are seriously injured or even killed in towns and villages. A majority of them are pedestrians or cyclists, who hardly have any protection to mitigate the consequences of the road accidents. On freeways, which represents only a small percent of the entire road network of Germany, road accidents with injured persons occur relatively often in relation to urban and non-urban environments in spite of simpler road characteristics. This can, however, be explained by the high usage of freeways, which is for Germany about one third of all kilometers driven.

IV. Challenges

For current advanced driver assistance systems available on the market, the automobile manufacturers are not yet taking full responsibility for the driving maneuvers automatically performed by the vehicles. This also applies to emergency functions like the Collision Mitigation System, which are usually to intervene only in case of critical situations. The interventions of the emergency functions are limited in time and thus their effects on the moving vehicle are also limited. During the usage of the comfort functions, the human driver

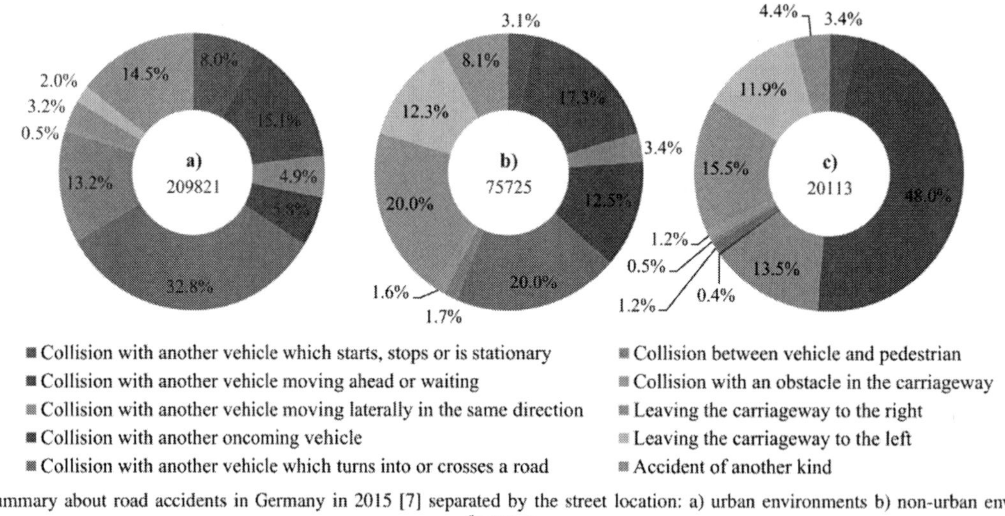

Figure 2. Summary about road accidents in Germany in 2015 [7] separated by the street location: a) urban environments b) non-urban environments c) freeways.

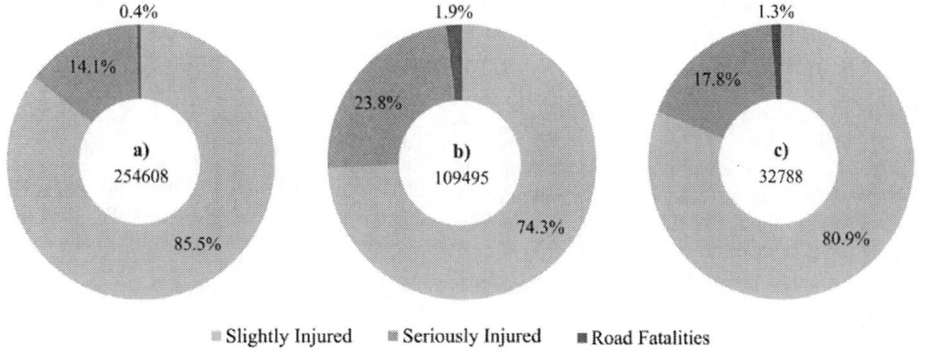

Figure 3. Summary about personal injuries caused by road accidents in Germany in 2015 [7] separated by the street location: a) urban environments b) non-urban environments c) freeways.

has to monitor the vehicle and to immediately take over the vehicle control in case of an unexpected system behavior. In the event of damage, she or he is fully responsible and not the automobile manufacture. Extensive test activities are performed, particularly in the premium segment, at test benches and with test vehicles to make sure that the human driver is left out as often as possible. Thereby, a balance between safety and availability must be found by the automobile manufactures. With automated driving, the automobile manufacturers are responsible as soon as they allow the human driver to be distracted towards the environmental conditions. Especially, the period of time until the human driver has taken over needs a closer look. Within this period of time, automated driving has to be maintained by the system. This means, e.g., that a takeover just before a collision, in which the driver has no possibility to avoid the collision, is not a suitable measure for handing over the vehicle control. Depending on the degree of distraction and the complexity of the current traffic situation, the necessary time until the takeover differs. In addition, characteristics of the human driver, e.g., the age and the mental state, play an essential role in the time required for the takeover of the vehicle control. The automobile manufacturers must assume that an appropriate time, which is expected to be in the double-digit seconds range [9], will be required after the notification.

The degradation of the functionality in case of automated driving is built on the assumption that the system knows its state and its operating limit at all times. On the basis of the current system state and the exact characteristic of the operating limit [10], the system can decide when and how it comes into a safe state in the event of a fault. A certain tolerance between the operating limit and the actually used limit for the degradation ensures thereby the robustness of the system, even if there are deviations due to certain tolerances of individual components. But in practice, it is difficult to determine any operating limit in advance for all traffic situations and to specify procedures to a safe system state that do not endanger the passengers or other road users. Moreover, the system has to predict its state to have enough time to react appropriately to a traffic situation that may only happen because of changes of the environmental conditions.

The previous sections argue that automated driving has the potential to save lives, which requires a correct operation of the system at all times and in any traffic situation without an immediate available human fallback level. State of the art test methods [11][12] are based on the approach that a certain selection of the system input represents the complete input range. Examples of such test methods are the Boundary Value Analysis, Equivalence Class Analysis and the Classification Tree Analysis. These approaches on the system input can reduce the number of tests tremendously. To apply such an approach, it is necessary that the test method divides the system input into classes in which the test object is expected to show the same response independently of the value taken out of the class. However, the classes are usually derived from the system requirements. Both, the requirement process and the derivation of the classes are human tasks and are therefore error-prone. In complex implementations with a large number of parameters, there might be branches implemented, which cannot be seen in the requirements. Even with systematic testing, it is sure that not every input pattern is tested, which can results in a misconduct of the system. As a worst case scenario, this misconduct can lead to a road accident, if it is either not compensated by the system itself or recognized and corrected by the human driver. Since the human driver is assumed to be distracted, the system either has to avoid such traffic situations or has to be able to cope with them, if they are in the period of time before the vehicle control is taken over.

According to [13], the test aim is transformed into an optimization problem in which the input of the test object creates the so called search space. The search space is a numeric representation for the possible stimulations that can be applied to the test object to obtain a response. For the obtaining of a specific system response, it is necessary to stimulate the system with the corresponding input pattern from the search space. The other way round, a specific input pattern from the search space causes a specific response of the system. Since automated driving algorithms are time variant, it is not sufficient to test only static input patterns, but also variations of the test scenarios that differ over the time. Changes in the timing of the input sequence can affect the system, e.g., feedback control loops. The same input sequence with a different timing might lead to a different response of the system. For this reason, it is proposed that the search space shall be divided into the following two parts:

a) Functional behavior
b) Temporal behavior

The consideration of the temporal behavior adds another

dimension to the functional system input many times over. However, the proposed separation between the functional and the temporal behavior allows a prioritization during the test execution. Thus, it is possible to test the functional behavior of the system at first followed by the testing of the temporal behavior. Especially, the temporal behavior is important for systems that are time-variant or have memories as explained in [14]. For this kind of systems, the times, e.g., at which a vehicle performs a specific action, are crucial factors.

Given the expected number of tests cases derived from the system input, a manual creation of the test cases is unfeasible. Common sense is that test case generators must be used for the test creation. The usage of test case generators multiplies the number of test cases, but not necessarily increases the quality of the tests or the covered search space. Generated test cases, which are redundant or outside the operating limit of the system, do not contribute to the improvement of the system. Hence, test case generators shall be optimized to focus on the relevant parts of the test object. Having said that, from a coverage point of view, many test cases are needed. It is to be stated that an execution of these test cases is only feasible, if the test execution is fully automated. This requirement is valid to both test generation and test execution. In contrast to today's available test case generators, which mostly leave the specification of the expected system response to the testers, they must be able to provide the system response based on the generated stimulation even for complex systems. But also the handling of the test execution takes a lot of time, if the allocation of the test cases to the test resources is not automated. A huge number of generated test cases require the corresponding amount of test resources, which can be optimized without human interaction. In summary, it can be said that the usage of test case generators leads to the following requirements:

a) Approaches to effectively use the test case generators for the automated driving domain
b) Test resources that are fully automated to increase the throughput
c) Scalable test resources to cope with the number of generated test cases
d) Test case generators that also provide the expected system behavior for the evaluation

V. Conclusion and Future Work

Already today, automation facilitates the driving and helps to reduce or even eliminate risks caused by human drivers. In contrast to emergency functions, which only intervene in critical traffic situations for a short period of time, the latest comfort functions temporarily take over the lateral and longitudinal control of the vehicle for specific driving scenarios. However, the human driver has to monitor the vehicle during the whole time to be immediately available as a fallback level in case of a system malfunction. The responsibility for the vehicle and possible damages lies with the human driver. With further steps in the direction of automated driving, the automobile manufacturers will have to assume the responsibility for the driving maneuvers automatically performed by the vehicles until the handover of the vehicle control to the human driver.

Automated driving, which does not endanger the passengers or other road users, can only be achieved, if the system recognizes its misconducts in case of failure well enough in advance to reach a safe state. To do this, it is necessary that the system knows its state and its operating limit at all times taking into account possible tolerances of the components. Moreover, the system has to predict its state to have enough time to react appropriately to a situation.

Automation of driving only has the potential to improve the traffic safety, if a correct operation of the system is ensured at all times and in any situation. Common test methods are based on human tasks and therefore error-prone. Even a systematic testing of the system does not allow that all possible combinations and timings of the system input can be tested and thus no misconduct exists. Thus, it is proposed by the presented approach to separate the functional and the temporal behavior of the system to enable a prioritization during the testing.

A mostly manual test process is unfeasible for automated driving due to the expected number of test cases required for the testing. Thus, the presented approach demands test resources that are fully automated to increase the throughput and scalability that compensate the increased test volume. Moreover, it further demands specialized test case generators for the automated driving domain that provide the expected system behavior for the evaluation based on the generated stimulation. Overall, an effective testing is necessary to cope with the challenges of automated driving.

It is left for future work to provide test methods, which have high search space coverages and can be used for an effective testing of the system behavior in different traffic situations. Furthermore, metrics are needed to obtain information about the system performance and the environmental conditions encountered during the test drives. It is thereby assumed that a single metric has no significance and that comparability can only be achieved by using several independent metrics if possible.

References

[1] SAE International, "Automated Driving - Levels of Driving Automation are Defined in New SAE International Standard J3016," 2014, [Online]. Available: https://www.sae.org/misc/pdfs/automated_driving.pdf [retrieved: March, 2017].

[2] NHTSA's National Center for Statistics and Analysis, "Critical Reasons for Crashes Investigated in the National Motor Vehicle Crash Causation Survey," 2015, [Online]. Available: https://crashstats.nhtsa.dot.gov/Api/Public/ViewPublication/812115 [retrieved: March, 2017].

[3] A. Zanten and F. Kost, Handbook of Driver Assistance Systems: Basic Information, Components and Systems for Active Safety and Comfort. Cham: Springer International Publishing, 2016, ch. Brake-Based Assistance Functions, pp. 919–967. [Online]. Available: http://dx.doi.org/10.1007/978-3-319-12352-3_40

[4] German Aerospace Center, "Research Project PEGASUS," URL: http://www.pegasus-projekt.info [retrieved: March, 2017].

[5] Fraunhofer Institute for Industrial Engineering IAO, "Highly Automated Driving on Freeways - Industrial Policy Conclusions ("Hochautomatisiertes Fahren auf Autobahnen Industriepolitische Schlussfolgerungen")," 2015, [Online]. Available: http://www.bmwi.de/Redaktion/DE/Downloads/H/hochautomatisiertes-fahren-auf-autobahnen.html [retrieved: March, 2017].

[6] H. Winner, W. Wachenfeld, and P. Junietz, "(How) Can Safety of Automated Driving be Validated?" 2016, [Online]. Available: http://www.fzd.tu-darmstadt.de/media/fachgebiet_fzd/publikationen_3/2016_5/2016_Wi_Wf_Ju_ViV-Symposium_Graz.pdf [retrieved: March, 2017].

[7] Federal Statistical Office of Germany, "Road Traffic Accidents - 2015 ("Verkehrsunfälle - 2015")," 2016, [Online]. Available: https://www.destatis.de/DE/Publikationen/Thematisch/TransportVerkehr/Verkehrsunfaelle/VerkehrsunfaelleJ2080700157004.html [retrieved: March, 2017].

[8] D. Rösler, "The relevance of traffic elements in driving situations definition, measurement, and application," Ph.D. dissertation, Chemnitz University of Technology, 2010. [Online]. Available: http://nbn-resolving.de/urn:nbn:de:bsz:ch1-201000403

[9] Gesamtverband der Deutschen Versicherungswirtschaft e.V., "Takeover times in highly automated driving - Compact accident research," 2016, [Online]. Available: https://udv.de/en/publications/compact-accident-research/takeover-times-highly-automated-driving [retrieved: March, 2017].

[10] A. T. Kleen, "Controllability of partially automated interventions in vehicle guidance ("Beherrschbarkeit von teilautomatisierten Eingriffen in die Fahrzeugführung")," Ph.D. dissertation, 2014. [Online]. Available: http://publikationsserver.tu-braunschweig.de/receive/dbbs_mods_00056694

[11] O. Bühler, "Evolutionary functional testing of embedded systems for distance-based automotive driver assistance functions ("Evolutionärer Funktionstest von eingebetteten Systemen für abstandsbasierte Fahrerassistenzfunktionen im Automobil")," Ph.D. dissertation, University of Tübingen, 2007.

[12] I. Jovanovic, "Software Testing Methods and Techniques," in The IPSI BgD Transactions on Internet Research, 2009, pp. 30–41. [Online]. Available: http://tir.ipsitransactions.org/2009/January/Full%20Journal.pdf

[13] F. Rothlauf, Optimization Problems. Berlin, Heidelberg: Springer Berlin Heidelberg, 2011, pp. 7–44. [Online]. Available: http://dx.doi.org/10.1007/978-3-540-72962-4_2

[14] S. Wittel, D. Ulmer, and O. Bühler, "Automatic Test Evaluation for Driving Scenarios Using Abstraction Level Constraints," in The Eighth International Conference on Advances in System Testing and Validation Lifecycle, 2016, pp. 14–19. [Online]. Available: http://www.thinkmind.org/index.php?view=article&articleid=valid_2016_2_20_40023

Evolving Agent Architecture for Data Collection

Ali Esserhir
LACL
Université Pars Est Créteil (UPEC)
Créteil, France
ali.esserhir@lacl.fr

Abstract— **The use of mobile agents has shown that agent migration is a solution for the change management. However, the use of such architecture is often quite complex, depending on the design approach. In this work, we propose to define a set of Rest (REpresentational State Transfer) interfaces for each element of our mobile agent architecture. Moreover, we have built a toolchain based on the small set of tools that allows the designer to easily update the facades of each element. Then, we apply our strategy for a validation of concept. A study is built about using mobile agents for data collection in a Rest architecture. We analyze our results and how we treat any changes in the design of our architecture.**

Keywords-software architecture; mobile agent; REST architecture; RESTful system.

I. INTRODUCTION

Nowadays, computer science projects have to deal with software architecture on one hand and agile methodology on the other side. By the end, we obtain a context where changes in architecture have a heavy impact on the lifecycle of the project. This topic is interesting since architecture and agile seem to have some conflicting forces at work. The definition of software architecture is a first challenge and the experts provide different visions about this concept. Our current definition is quite common, but explicit: software architecture is the collection of decisions affecting the system's quality attributes, which have global effects and are hardest to change.

As a precision, software architecture provides the frame within which the design is built by the developers. Because a component diagram often describes an architecture, the component definition is essential. In our work, it is an autonomous part of our software, which exposes a public interface and needs outside interface for working. B. Wallace introduces the idea that a component definition cannot exist without a framework selection [1]. For Rainer Niekamp, a component is first a reusable unit of software, which is able to communicate with other components via interfaces [2]. Raphael Gfeller considers a component as an administrable entity into a software project with dependencies and features [3]. All these definitions depict different facets of what is a component. In addition, we consider that, when a software architecture evolves, it is crucial that all its components are administrable and exchangeable through well-defined interfaces under the control of a selection of specifications or frameworks.

On the client side, the invocation way of a component must be as simple as a local method call. R. Fielding has worked on this problem and his REST philosophy is welcomed in many projects, regardless of the programming language is used. Such simplicity had already been applied which the SOA (Service-Oriented Architecture) architecture with the use of ESB (Enterprise Service Bus) framework like Apache ServiceMix [4]. This framework requires the use of VETO pattern for the treatment of the client requests.

Moreover, to manage the complexity of evolving a software-distributed system, its architecture description has to be linked through an accurate and traceable way to its implementation. Too often, only the software architect is able to maintain the software architecture and no one knows the keys for updating the architecture. The software architecture deals with multiple views of a system, including both its functional and nonfunctional facets. A structural approach looks at the system as a set of components that interact via interfaces. Complexity is mastered by means of hierarchical decomposition; a component can be composed of subcomponents with the hierarchy's leaf components representing coded functionality. As the Architecture Description Languages (ADL) group describes, this research community has proposed numerous ADL versions [5].

Any software-distributed system is constantly subject to software changes, usually driven by external constraints from the runtime environment over which the developers have no control at all. These constraints may be as diverse and unpredictable as technological changes, enhanced user organizational structures or business processes, new legislation, or changes in resources. To cope with any of these issues, all software artifacts produced and used by the software-distributed system have to evolve. Depending on the software artifacts' type, the impact and rate of change may differ. Evolving a software architecture by modifying its description to accommodate change requests faces numerous research challenges. In particular, the evolution of an architectural description should typically preserve its purpose and criticality concerns. However, often, the clients express the changes and it is not a set of bug fixes. In addition, the checks are on the preservation of the existing architecture.

Our work is about the lifecycle of the architectural changes and, more precisely, in the context of Resource Oriented Architecture (ROA) architecture. This acronym is created by the Django framework [6] and is now used for designing a software architecture based on REST concepts. It requires that all components are accessible through a REST API (Application Programming Interface).

This document is structured into several sections. Section 1 is around the topic of the evolving architecture for collecting data. Section 2 is about the related works, which are closed to our topic. Section 3 is on the use of mobile agent for the management of changes. In Section 4, we explain how our four-step strategy pilots the development process of the changes of a component. In Section 5, we apply this process for a case study on data collection over a network. In Section 6, we detail our results and analyze the reasons of the success of such approach. Finally, in Section 7, we summarize the main results of our contribution.

II. RELATED WORK

The software architecture field is often considered too abstract or too technical. Software architecture includes the global control structures, protocols for communication, synchronization, physical distribution, scaling and performance, and selection among design alternatives.

A. Agent architecture

One of the alternatives in the design of the software architecture is how to access remote resources or make calls to remote objects; or how to send the program code over the network. Four different paradigms have been identified: Client-Server, Remote Evaluation, Code on Demand, Mobile Agents. In this case, the code, including its execution state and some of its resources, is sent to a remote site where it executes. It can continue to another site if needed.

In order to make a mobile agent system work, it is not enough to build the agents themselves. A program at each site is also needed to handle the incoming agents and send out agents. This program is often called an agent factory. The agent factory can be built differently depending on which type of agent system is needed. The generic mobile agent system can have a range of varying components. It needs a communication module that handles incoming and outgoing agents, as well as the messaging between non-local agents. It has a repository that performs authentication, sets priorities and queues up agents for later execution.

One of the first ideas was to use mobile agents for searching through the Internet for the lowest prices of products and services. While the idea was good in theory, few companies wanted other people's agents in their computers, not only for security reasons, but probably for marketing reasons, too. They wanted people to come to their place and keep them there. Another domain is remote control, where applications are intended to control or reprogram remote computers, devices or unmanned vehicles by sending agents with new commands or program updates. These updates can be done very quickly, making it very good for applying security patches. Agents can also be used for monitoring devices and reporting back when status changes or problems occur, or can even be used for intrusion detection and active defense of computer systems [7]. A similar example of remote control is an abstraction called Mobile Streams [14]. Using that system, a distributed, event-driven application can be scripted from a single point of control and dynamically extended and reconfigured during execution.

Another application area for mobile agents or simply mobile code is to dynamically program the networks themselves in order to make them more flexible, customized and give them higher performance. At the lower level, the network devices like routers and switches can be remotely programmed [8] by sending mobile code which can change the topology and routing [9]. Instead of being passive, the networks become more active by taking a certain part in the computations or filtering the data [10].

Instead of doing all the processing and computations on a central computer, they can be distributed to several computers in a network. It is somewhat similar to process migration, but the difference is that processes usually migrate within a tightly coupled unit with several synchronized processors. The code is distributed to the remote computer to do the filtering and processing locally. This often reduces the network traffic and is a way to balance the load of computers with different capacities. It can also be more redundant when several computers do the same processing and the results can be compared. The agent migration allows the agent hosts for receiving updates of their business code without any service stop and the clients cannot observe any interruption of services. What stays difficult is the agent factory interface. Often, it is written in a specific programming language and its use from a given project needs to write new wrapper technical code. Also, developers and architects prefer the use of interoperable API over a standard protocol like http.

B. REST API definition and restful system

We have studied many architectures before choosing REST architecture. We have found that this architecture is the most suitable for data collecting by mobile agent. We will see below what is à REST architecture.

Roy Thomas Fielding defined REST in his 2000 PhD dissertation "Architectural Styles and the Design of Network-based Software Architectures". REST-compliant Web services allow requesting systems to access and manipulate textual representations of Web resources using a uniform and predefined set of stateless operations.

A web service must respect 6 constraints in order to be a Restful system:

- Client-Server: there must be a separation between server and client (separation of concerns)
- Stateless: Client does not conserve any client contest between two requests.
- Cacheable: Clients and intermediaries can cache responses
- Layered system: Requires that this middleware be inserted transparently, so that interaction between a given service and consumer is consistent, regardless of whether the consumer is communicating with a service residing in a middleware layer or a service that represents the ultimate receiver of a message.
- Code on demand (optional): Servers can temporarily extend or customize the functionality of a client by the transfer of executable code.

- Uniform interface: The uniform interface constraint is fundamental to the design of any REST service. The uniform interface simplifies and decouples the architecture, which enables each part to evolve independently. Uniform interface have four constraints:
  - Identification of resources
  - Manipulation of resources through representations
  - Self-descriptive messages
  - Hypermedia as the engine of application

III. Evolving Architecture Based on Mobile Agents

We have already used mobile agents in our previous work. Because technologies evolves quickly, the way we implemented such this software concept changes also following the discovery of more suitable frameworks. The main concepts are unchanged like, an agent factory, an agent server, a registry of agents and so on, but the technical aspects are more or less hidden to the developers and the users.

A. What is an evolution in an agent architecture ?

When a mobile agent architecture is deployed, a mobile agent imports a behavior and data from an agent server to an agent host. In addition, this host is enriched at runtime with the incoming agents. In the context of network control, a mobile agent can reconfigure an agent host with the import of updated features such that the address of the mail server, the connection string to a database, the name of the persistence unit.

Another application domain is the data collection where a mobile agent or a set of mobile agents walk through the agent hosts and collect useful data such that the log files, the updates of a NoSQL database, etc. Back to the agent server, the collected data are parsed, and actions are planned depending on their semantics. This means that a main database is updated, or some piece of code is applied on the log file to detect the anomalies at runtime (post analysis).

To summarize, we consider a configured mobile agent as a concrete evolution into a mobile agent system. This evolution will be considered when this mobile agent would have browsed the interested agent hosts.

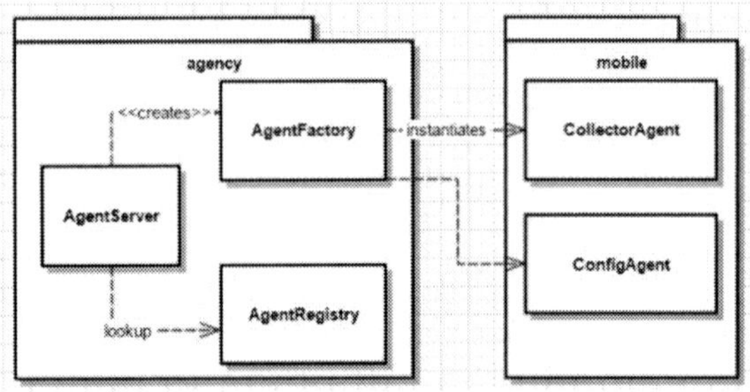

Figure 1. Overview of a mobile agent architecture.

Figure 1 shows the main elements of a mobile agent architecture. The agent server receives all the client requests and depending on the previous demands; it finds a mobile agent, which is already instantiated into the agent registry or it asks the agent factory for creating a new mobile agent. Then, it configures the mobile agent depending on the incoming request. This scenario describes a strategy called AOD. This is useful when the agent hosts know their need or when they know that a part of their knowledge is obsolete. Often, the hosts are not requestor and they do not know that they need of a refresh event.

This second scenario considers another mobile agent strategy called Proactive. It means that a mobile agent has to propagate the updates without any demand from the hosts. In addition, it knows a list of destination and sequentially it updates each host identified by its uniform resource location. Of course, the hosts should have been first configured to accept any mobile agents. We do not consider the security aspect in this document but it appears obvious that this has to be enforced in a professional context. When the mobile agent finishes its mission, then it comes back to the agent server and provides a report about its activities on each host. This involves new actions from the server. It can shut off a host or restart it with a minimal configuration, etc.

We have considered only one mobile agent in action, but we can improve the implementation of the evolution with the launch of several mobile agent concurrently. In that context, the mobile agent needs to exchange messages at runtime. The use of messages allows reducing the migration of agent. In some situation, it allows the validation of a mobile agent activity. For instance, when a mobile agent configures the REST interface of an agent host, then a remote agent can test whether the availability of this interface is ok. To sum up, we note that different types of mobile agent implement an evolution through the browsing of the hosts. Each of them contribute to the satisfaction of the whole mission, this include the validation of the activity and the generation of reports by the end. In both scenarios, the reuse of agent is done with the use of a registry.

B. Self adaptation system

Today, the adaptation of a system is a crucial property for the lifetime of an application. The adaptation is necessary not only because of the aging of a software, but also because the resources are limited in all contexts. In software, we have to consider that the memory is finite, the run time has to be under a threshold required by a product owner and the energy cost has to be also under a given consumption. When a limit is achieved, the system has to adapt its behavior for avoiding a global failure. Aldo, in that context we have already experimented that a mobile agent architecture is a solution. For instance, in an embedded context (mobile phone, tablet, etc.), it is thrifty to move the back end of a mobile application to an application server and keep only the front end with the graphical user interface on the mobile device.

The transfer of data is quite common but in case of mobile agent, the import of code is under security constraints. Therefore, an agent loader receives a byte code stream, converts it into a local agent, and then run it. We consider this operation as an access to a remote resource. We implement this network importation as a message exchange pattern based on request / response schema. The content of the message is the code of the mobile agent and its current state. Moreover, because of the security rules, the vehicle of our message is the http protocol. These technical choices are not too restrictive and allow several message formats depending on the frameworks.

This means that all the elements of our architecture (Figure 1) respect a Facade design pattern where all the remote operations are exposed to their future clients. Although, this involve that new operations could appear at runtime depending on where the mobile agents could be or depending on the scheduling of an evolution. We clearly separate the migration concern form the implementation of the evolution and this stresses the inner structure of a mobile agent. It is a composite based on several parts.

At a first level, a mobile agent implements a contract, which is used at the top abstraction of a proxy pattern (Figure 2). Since the agent proxy and agent behavior both implement AgentResource, it allows the client to treat the

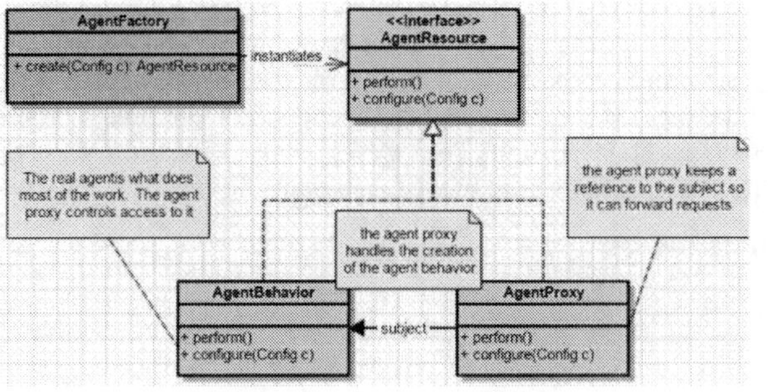

Figure 2. Mobile agent structure.

proxy like the AgentBehavior. An agent host loads such agent and depending on the implemented strategy, its activity is run by a call of perform method.

IV. FOUR STEP LIFECYLE

We apply an incremental project lifecycle divided into 4 steps: agent analysis, agent design, agent development and agent validation. This lifecycle unit is repeated until the end of a distributed project. In the following sections, we detail the definition of the REST interfaces of all the elements of our distributed system based on mobile agents.

A. Agent system analysis

The analysis system means that we define rigorously the facade of each element of our system. It starts with the naming of the elements and their public interface with a signature. A suitable approach consists in the construction of an interaction diagram that describes how a group of objects collaborates in some behavior. Typically, a single use-case has an execution, which is described by this sequence of interaction. The diagrams show a number of example objects and the messages that are passed between these objects within the use-case. It is difficult to write much about interaction diagrams because they are so simple. However, they have weaknesses; the main one is that although they are good at describing behavior: they do not define it. They typically do not show all the iteration and control that is needed to give a computationally complete description.

A first reading of such sequence diagram provides the naming of methods and parameters, with potential types. Jacobson uses pseudo-code in conjunction with sequence charts to provide a more executable model. Others have added various diagrammatic notations to increase the model's usability. Many of these are included in the UML notation. We adopted a standard open software for the construction of such diagrams like the online tool called web sequence diagram. Because a use case can have several distinct executions, we create more than one sequence diagrams. By the end of the analysis step, we create all the façade of the project.

B. REST API design

The design of the mobile agent interfaces consists in a deeper reading of the previous sequence diagrams and the selection of a more rigorous language for a more precise description. He has selected the Swagger language for such description. Its goal is to define a standard, language-agnostic interface to REST APIs. It allows both humans and computers to discover and understand the capabilities of the service without access to source code, documentation.

Swagger is a formal specification surrounded by a large ecosystem of tools, which includes everything from front-end user interfaces, low-level code libraries and commercial API management solutions. In addition, from a Swagger specification, it is possible to create the service implementations and the client parts.

First, a Swagger specification file allows us to describe an API including:

- General information about the API
- Available paths or resource naming (/resources)
- Available operations on each path http verbs (get /resources)
- Input/output for each operation and message format.

Once written, OpenAPI specification file contains the description of a data model and all the supported operations. It can also be used as:

- source material for documentation
- specification for developers
- partial or complete code generation
- and many other things such as analysis and diagram generation

C. Skeleton generation and business delegate pattern

Because code generation means a framework selection, our previous experiments lead us to choose Spring framework for the service implementation. The principle consists in the separation of concern and the use of the Business Delegate pattern. It means that the business code does not belong to the service but it is called from the service implementation. The swagger code generator project, allows the generation of API client libraries (SDK generation), server stubs and documentation automatically given a YAML specification.

Because of the code generation, the developer obtains a Maven project with a pom.xml file. This file descriptor contains all the knowledge of the project, its dependencies, the useful build plugins and the report plugins. Maven requires respecting its own lifecycle for the installation of the project. Some user modifications are necessary into this file descriptor to adapt the code generation to the user platform. Then a run of the project exposes the main uniform resource location to the public. When the application is launched locally to a server, then a possible URL is as follows:

http://localhost:8080/v1

The response is a web page where all the operations are proposed and a documentation page is displayed for all the users. Therefore, a user can browse all the operations and read the textual contract. This page allows him to create basic test request by the use of specific forms.

This step contains also the generation of clients. In that context, it means, the client for each element of our architecture. These clients support the invocation process described in Section 3 about the agent lookup into a registry and the agent creation from the agent factory interface. For the same reason, we selected Spring framework for the client part and based on this result we can build our own agent strategy.

D. Test and validation based on Exchange pattern

Validation is determining whether the system complies with the requirements and performs treatments for which it is intended. In addition, it meets the organization's goals and user needs. Of course, this step does not contain a large set of requests sent manually to the services. We use also a framework for the test build. SmartBear is the editor of SOAPUI application that is a standard in the validation domain. This means that from an interface definition, it is able to build template of requests and then it submits them. By the end, it compares an expected result with an actual result.

Instead of spinning up a new browser tab, typing into a slick user interface and clicking buttons, we reached for a tool and thought carefully about data and endpoint paths. When we test an API, we deal with the stuff under the covers and the framework called REST API Testing offers all these concepts. Therefore, we are able to test each REST interface of our architecture and we can create script where the interfaces are composed to validate our strategy of architecture adaptation. We used this approach for the demand of a new data collection to the agent server.

We use also the Swagger Test Templates (STT) module, through either the command line interface or programmatically. It generates a robust, end-to-end testing suite for all a developer's API endpoints defined in their Swagger specification. Then we are able to fill some parts of the code with specific assertions about the business data we

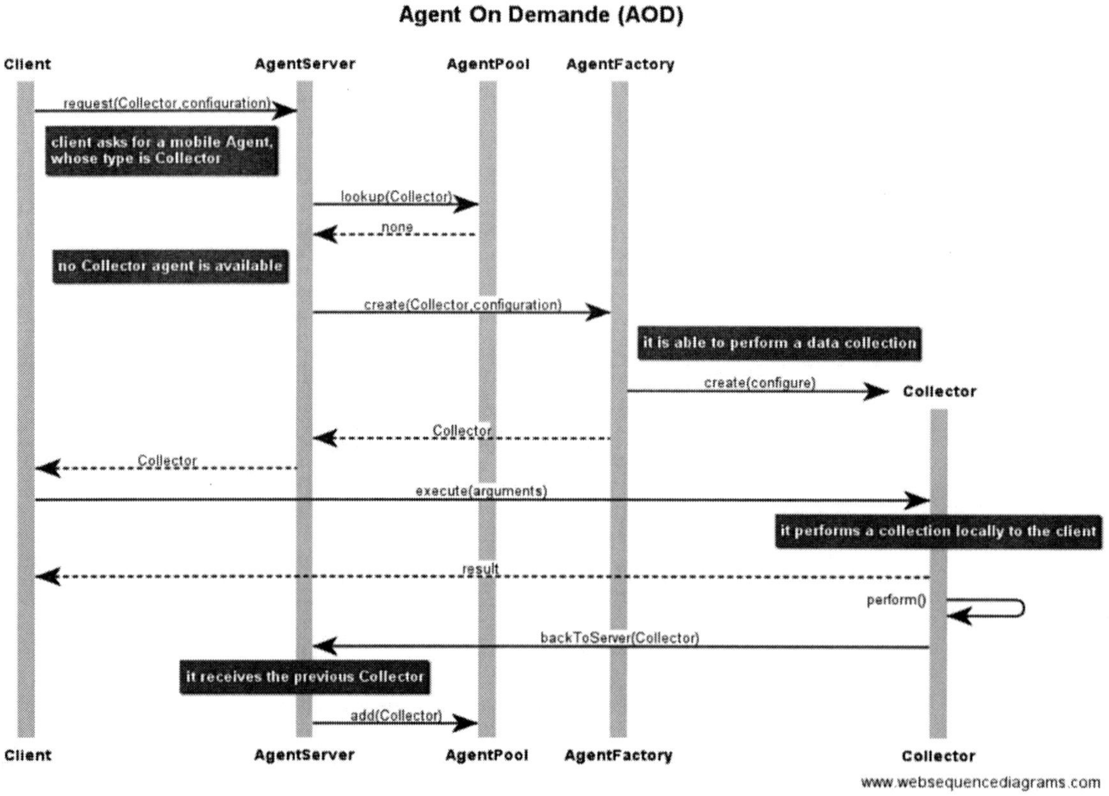

Figure 3. Sequence Diagram : Agent On Demand

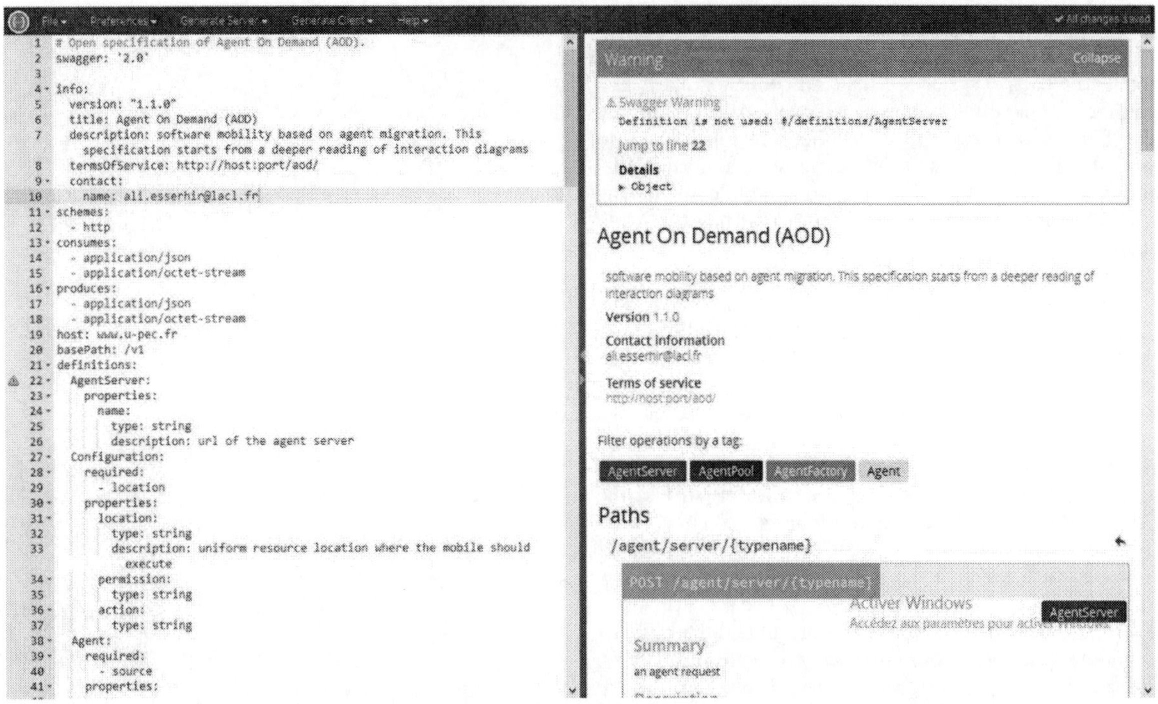

Figure 4. Open specification for an agent server

want to send. This saves hours of test writing and enables us to quickly deploy on our server a suitable version of all the REST services.

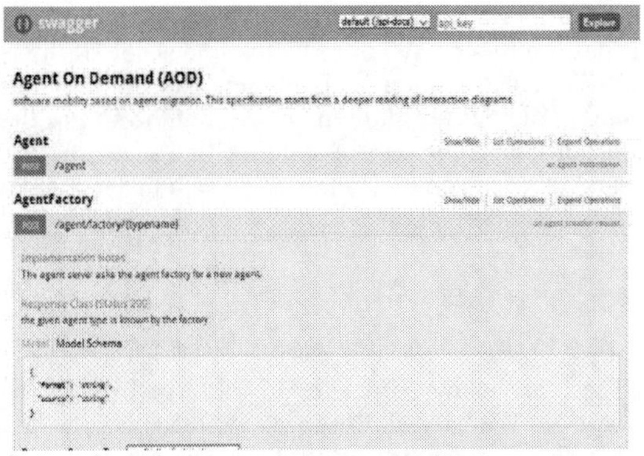

Figure 5. Agent interface generation

After finishing writing the specification of REST Web services, we generate a server and a client using the tool provided by Swagger. In this way, we can test our REST web services (in Figure 5).

V. Case Study

A. Agent sequence diagram

The sequence diagram In Figure 3 describes the way that a client asks an AgentServer for an agent able to collect data.

B. Open specification for an agent system

We have used Open specification, in order to specify our REST web services, Swagger tool offer an online "Swagger editor". We have used Yaml language for specifying our API. In Figure 4 we can see on the left side the Yaml code we have written, and on the right side, the documentation generated by Swagger.

C. Agent interface generation and packaging

VI. Analysis and Results

Our scenario is a brief narrative description of a system to capture relevant information for computer health and problem management monitoring. For example, practice management systems manage the business of the general practice by recording computer details, managing application servers and database system.

A. Scenario on data collection

The data collection covers a network of computers where log files are saved. They describe the health of application servers and database systems. This data collection starts at a given time and the process is repeated every day. The format of the files is text and the collection principle means to append the file of the same structure into a master file. Behind a file format, there is at least one mobile agent. The number of agents depends on the number of hosts to walk through.

In our test scenario, we consider per computer a JBoss Server as the application server, and a MySQL server. The application server contains many tools, which configured to work together. Several log files are touched by the data collections. The configuration of the database server set features for a verbose mode and the trace of SQL statements with all database events. The locations of the log files are known paths when the installation is done successfully. To sum up, this scenario groups 8 kind of file format and the size of the files depends on the activity of the servers.

Before starting the scenario, all the agent hosts install permissions for accepting the mobile agents of our factory and for executing a file reading operation. The scenario starts with a request to the agent server (Figure 1) and the build of 8 mobile agents. Their configurations come from .ini files, which are read, by the agent factory. Next, the factory registers the mobile agents and the agent server launches the mission of each agent sequentially. Each mobile agent contains the route of computers where it has to perform its data collection. Because each agent host has a remote interface for accepting such mobile agent, then a mobile agent invokes the first host of its list and if automatically installed into the virtual machine of the host. Then it reads the set of files, which corresponds to the file format it knows and leaves the agent host for the next host in its list. When all the items of the list are visited, the mobile agent comes back to the server where its data are consumed and parsed. The test contains 6 computers with two servers to manage.

The whole data collection is finished when all the mobile agents are back to the server and their data depose in the corresponding folder. Another part of the scenario starts with the analysis of text patterns and the recognition of abnormal events or durations that are greater than expected. The consequence could the restart of services, which belong to a computer or the final stop in case of high gravity.

B. Events and time

In addition to the business data collection, a mobile agent records its own activity. Each import or export event is recorded with time. The route followed by an agent can be observed during its course by JMX components (Java Management eXtension).

Our first results are about the collected data size. A mobile agent browses 6 nodes (or computers). This means that an agent appends six log files (about 200 kbytes) in the current test and the time cost is near 140 ms. When the data collection occurs too early, the time results are not meaningful, because the size of the data has consequences on the duration of the course.

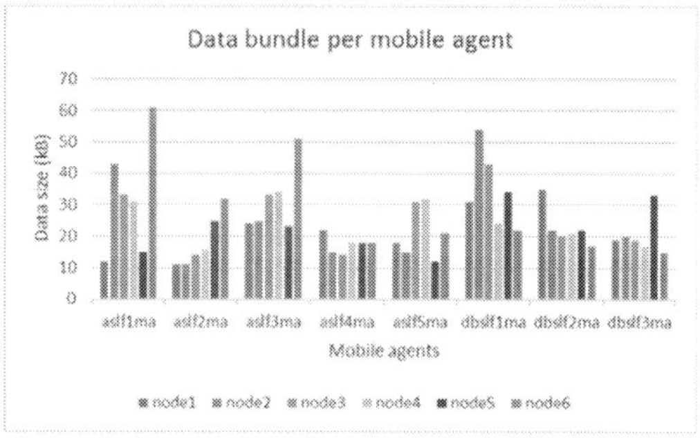

Figure 6. Data size per mobile agent.

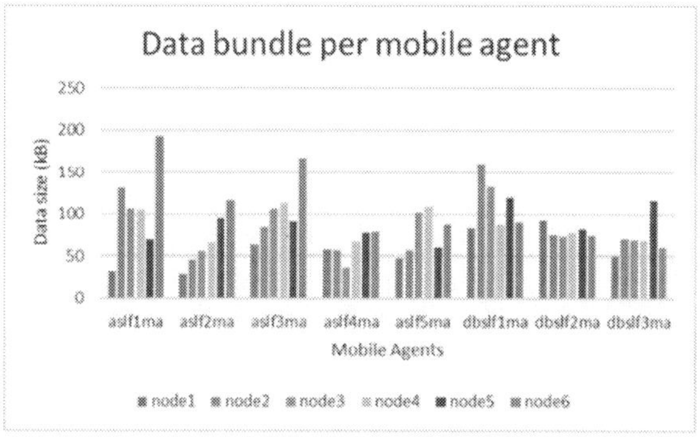

Figure 7. Data size per mobile agent.

So, we rebuild the same scenario another time but after an intensive activity period. We use Apache JMeter for increasing the number of requests and this involves more traffic on the database server.

During the second test, the activity has increased and the log files are bigger. We observe that the shape of the results is similar but the duration is bigger than the previous one (524ms). The ratio is more than three but the size of the data is a quadruple in comparison with the first scenario. We have pursued this benchmark (in Figure 7) with this metric and we confirm this observation.

VII. CONCLUSION AND FUTURE WORKS

There are many parameters to observe in such kind of application. We have shown that mobile agent is well suited for building a dynamic architecture. The automatize design and build of REST interfaces is another key result of our work. We consider that our project could help other designers to convince that the building of a REST layer can be done in a very predictive time.

We want to continue our measures and more precisely the cost of a couple of actions import/export. We would like to show that a mobile agent a good approach for the reactive systems, especially in the control of network and its administration.

REFERENCES

[1] R. B. Wallace, R. M. Dansereau, and R. A. Goubran: "Methods for the detection of ECG characteristic points". MeMeA 2012: pp. 1-6

[2] M. Krosche, R. Niekamp, and H. G. Matthies: "A Component Based Architecture for Coupling Optimization and Simulation Software in a Distributed Environment". SNPD 2003: pp. 20-23

[3] R. Gfeller and P. Hauser: "Rotated Lines - A Heatmap Representation Method for People Affected by any Kind of Color Blindness". Mensch & Computer 2010: pp. 235-240

[4] F. Amato and F. Moscato: "Exploiting Cloud and Workflow Patterns for the Analysis of Composite Cloud Services". Future Generation Comp. Syst. 67: pp. 255-265 2017

[5] E. S. de Almeida and F. Oquendo: "Software Components, Architectures and ReuseModeling, Customization and Evaluation". J. UCS 19(2): pp. 183-185 2013.

[6] A. Lenk, M. Menzel, J. Lipsky, S. Tai, and P. Offermann: "What Are You Paying For? Performance Benchmarking for Infrastructure-as-a-Service Offerings". IEEE CLOUD 2011: pp. 484-491

[7] S. Bayati, A. K. Tripathi: "Designing a Knowledge Base for OSS Project Recommender System: a Big Data Analytics Approach". ECIS 2016: Research-in-Progress Paper 37

[8] K. Ranganathan and S. Arora: "Enabling Grassroots Communication: A Memory-Aided Broadcast Mechanism for a Community Radio Service on an Ad hoc Device-to-Device Mobile Network". IEEE Trans. Communications 62(3): pp. 1138-1150 2014

[9] D. P. Bertsekas: "Robust Shortest Path Planning and Semicontractive Dynamic Programming". CoRR abs/1608.01670 2016.

[10] L. Wang, X. Wang, and T. S. T. Mak: "Adaptive Routing Algorithms for Lifetime Reliability Optimization in Network-on-Chip". IEEE Trans. Computers 65(9): pp. 2896-2902 2016.

Design of Mobile Services for Embedded Device

Guy Lahlou Djiken
Laboratory of Algorithms,
Complexity and Logics,
LACL, UPEC University
Créteil, France
guy-lahlou.djiken@lacl.fr

Sanae Mostadi
Ecole Supérieure d'Informatique
Appliquée à la Gestion,
ESIAG, UPEC University
Créteil, France
mostadis@miage.u-pec.fr

Fabrice Mourlin
Laboratory of Algorithms,
Complexity and Logics,
LACL, UPEC University
Créteil, France
fabrice.mourlin@u-pec.fr

Abstract—**The design of distributed applications requires theoretical knowledge and hands-on experience. Our work is about distributed applications based on embedded platforms, such as smartphones or tablets. We define a software chain development from design to implementation where services are designed through interface diagrams and component diagrams. From these declarations, we are able to generate software descriptions into two languages. Android Interface Description Language (AIDL) is utilized for local services to an embedded platform. Web Application Description Language (WADL) is utilized for remote services. Such services are called from one platform to another one. The first kind of description allows developers to create Android services. Then, WADL description provides all the features for building Restlet Web services. We applied our strategy to the design and building of a case study on medical picture set management. Embedded tablets can take pictures during the users' activities. Local services allow users to display their medical picture through specific viewers. Remote services are set to expose these data to specific medical material. So, we provided a way to exchange technical data from well spread platforms to medical application servers.**

Keywords-mobility; data collection; mobile service; distributed application.

I. INTRODUCTION

Tanenbaum defines a distributed system as a "*collection of independent computers that appear to the users of the system as a single computer*". This means that two features are essential: independent and suitable software for hiding the architecture from the users [1].

We consider a distributed system as a collection of autonomous computers linked by a network and using software to produce an integrated computing facility. The size of a distributed system can belong to a local area network (10's of hosts) or a metropolitan area network (100's of hosts) or a wide area network (internet) (1000's or 1,000,000's of hosts). The key characteristics of such distributed systems are the resource sharing, where data source or external device are used by applications. Then, the use of open standard allows to build applications which need to have the components of a solution work together [2]. The concurrency property is also important in the fact that multiple activities are executed at the same time [3]. This reduces latency and allows to hide blocking with some computing.

The scalability in size deals with large numbers of machines, users, tasks, etc. This property also occurs in a location with geometric distribution and mobility [4]. The subject of our work is the design of distributed applications based on services. When considering a scalable application design, a service helps to decouple functionality and thinks about each part of the application as its own service with a clearly defined interface. For SOA application (Service Oriented Architecture), each service has its own distinct functional context, and interaction with anything outside of that context takes place through an abstract interface, typically the public-facing API of another service.

Building a system on a set of complementary services decouples the operation of those pieces from one another. This abstraction helps establish clear relationships between the services, its underlying environment, and the consumers of that service. Our work is about the use of services, which are Web services or embedded services. Both types occur in real projects, and it seems to be essential to adopt the same design approach. Section II describes our methodology for specifying both types of services. Section III is about the use of intermediate representation between design charts and computer representations. The following section is about a way to provide an implementation. In the last two sections we describe a case study and we built on the management of the pictures with their localization. Finally, we summarize the results explained in this paper.

II. DESIGN OF DISTRIBUTED SERVICES

Client/server, 3-tier and n-tier distributed applications and cloud computing, open up new opportunities and ways to design systems and develop applications. The design challenge is the main step of the life cycle of any project. The definition of message exchange pattern is essential for the declaration of each remote service. An object-oriented modelling approach is often used to describe business requirements, identify components, their interactions and placement in a multi-tier environment.

We have chosen UML description language [5] as a specification language. There are a lot of charts which can help designers perform requirement specification. We have selected a deployment diagram for architecture level and how materials are linked. Next, the use of component diagram is the core of our methodology with the specification of interfaces and the declaration of signatures.

A. Design step of distributed services

1) A service approach

Similar to other distributed applications, Web services have a specific structure and behavior. The structure is the static part of Web services, which is composed of the candidate classes and their associations. The behavior is called the dynamic part. It represents how the Web service are executed in terms of sending requests, preparing responses to these requests, and how they will be sent back to the clients.

The Unified Modelling Language (UML) [5] gains greater acceptance among software designers, not only because of its standardization by the Object Management Group (OMG) [10], but also because of the high support from tool vendors, such as IBM and Oracle.

2) First step in our case study

Throughout our paper, we use a case study about the management of pictures which are taken with mobile devices such as smartphones and tablets. The main goal for an end user is to know precisely where a given picture is. More precisely, if several devices are used in a lab, it could be convenient to localize the pictures on the devices without any upload of working pictures on a common data server.

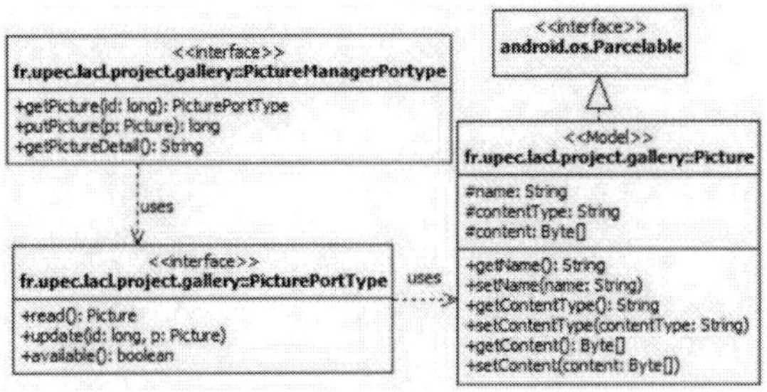

Figure 1. Precise declaration of interface and signature

The main goal of the Web service requirements analysis task is to capture and gather the requirements for the target Web service. This includes the identification of the precise services that have to be provided. This means that UML interfaces are defined in a package structure. For instance, assume a context where a set of pictures has to be exposed to a network with HTTP methods. So, Figure 1 will be the first step of the requirement specification.

This short example stresses 2 main tasks: the naming and the signature definition. Type and name of the domain and co-domain are essential to the future implementation and the clients. All these definitions are relative to a namespace (in our example `fr.upec.lacl.project.gallery`). This allows reducing name conflict. A package structure is an ideal entry point into a project dictionary.

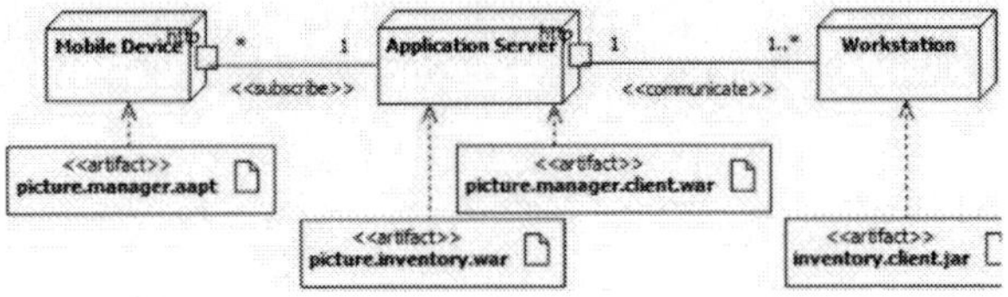

Figure 2. Deployment diagram

On the other hand, a material description provides all the details useful for the deployment step. In our previous example, the occurrences of the service are deployed on mobile devices. The clients could also be installed on mobile platforms or workstations. In Figure 2, a potential deployment diagram is described as a mobile application server deployed over a mobile device. Its client is installed on an application server. When all data are collected about the pictures, the other artifact, called picture.inventory.war deployed over the application server, can answer the requests of the standard clients.

From this view, we define several artifacts. They play the role of deliverables. Each of them will provide one or more components. A component diagram gives a snapshot of a runtime. Each component has provided interfaces and also dependencies on other parts of the software. Also, we can check how precisely the requirements are defined. This allows defining the used network protocol and the message exchange pattern. For instance, the requests to the `PictureManager` service is considered synchronous and parameters are exchanged through an XML format

This component diagram is also the support to express no functional properties, such that the maintainability of the set of services and the management of several versions. All the components follow the OSGi specification (Open Service Gateway Interface). A feature of OSGi technology is its portability, since it can be implemented both in the terminal board as well as in conventional applications or servers [6]. In this context, the OSGi technology is designed to address the other non-functional aspects, such that to enable the management of complex applications and to improve the quality of service applications for administration at runtime; see Figure 3.

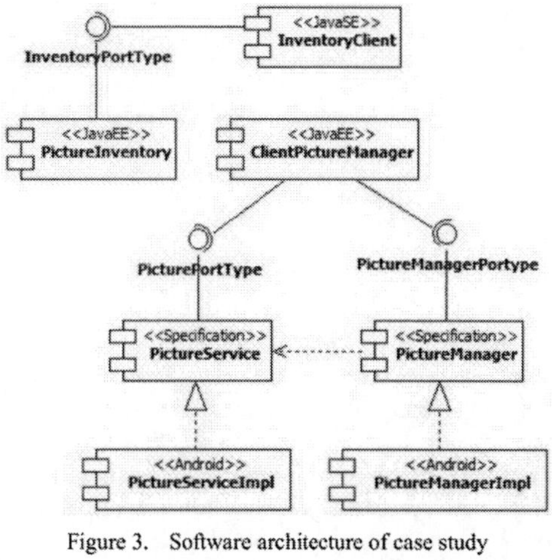

Figure 3. Software architecture of case study

In Figure 3, all components are placed. The naming convention allows readers to understand the correspondence between components and artifacts. There are three kinds of components depending on the kind of deployment node. This diagram highlights the roadmap of our development. So, because Figure 2 requires different kinds of platforms, then, the next refinements are going to provide more details about the technical features.

B. Integration testing

The integration testing is a level of the software testing process where individual units are combined and tested as a group. The purpose of this level of testing is to expose faults in the interaction between integrated units. In our context, it means the integration of the three parts: mobile part, server part and a client part. This level of test can be considered as business routes where each of them is a use of our distributed application. In Figure 4, we describe the integration scenario where the application server sends requests to mobile platforms and collects the URLs of pictures and their technical features.

This sequence diagram plays the role of validation after the integration of all the components and their deployment on to the set of materials.

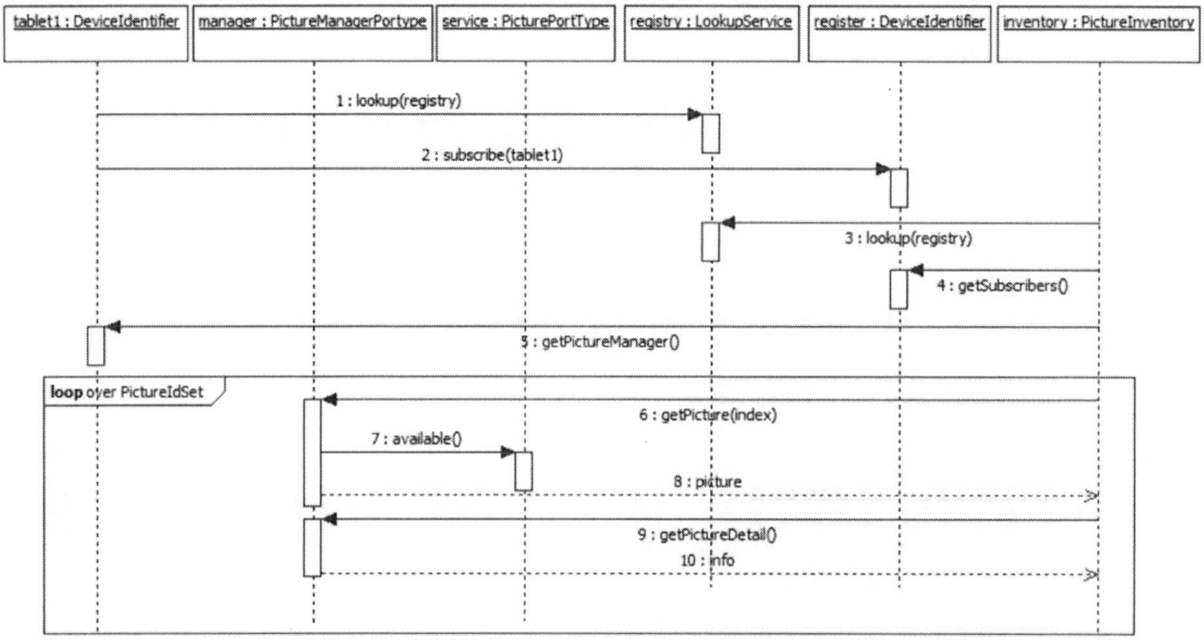

Figure 4. Interaction diagram as integration test

We also use such kind of diagrams when we study the impact of a scenario on the other behaviors of the application server. For instance, the problem can be to understand what the consequences of the data collections are during the subscription of other mobile devices. It seems to be obvious to require that the main business functionalities have to be isolated and the use of one mobile device is independent from the use of another one.

Figure 4 shows the interactions between a tablet and the application server. First, the mobile device is registered and a collector service validates the availability of all the data around the pictures (content, format, identification, localization, etc.). This diagram can be extended with the introduction of other mobile devices or the interaction with other scenarios, but this will introduce some noise into the description and the role of such diagram will be reduced.

III. INTERMEDIATE REPRESENTATION

From the previous set of diagrams, we have to continue towards a more technical representation. As we can observe, this distributed application is based on the use of remote service. These services are clearly defined and, depending on the kind of platform, we use a precise approach.

A. AIDL services

The IDL (Interface Definition Language) [7] is generally language independent for the service specification. It is used theoretically for generating C++ or Python stub code from it. The Android one is Java-based though, so the distinction is subtle. One difference is that there is only a single interface in an .aidl file, while Java allows multiple classes/interfaces per Java file. There are also some rules for which types are supported, so it is not exactly the same as a Java interface, and it is not allowed to use one instead of AIDL.

In the context of mobile programming, a service is an application component that runs in the background without a user interface. In our case study, the picture manager can perform data collection by using a background service to prepare data for a foreground application. This means another application of the mobile device. This is quite important because the consequence is that a service built from AIDL cannot be used remotely.

Services work in the background, even though the application is running neither in foreground nor in the background. A service might handle long running tasks like network connections or retrieving database records with the help of a content provider from the background. In our case study, two interfaces are defined to expose services on the mobile platform: these are `PictureManagerPortType` and `PicturePortType`; see Figure 1. So from these declarations, we transform them into two .aidl files.

These files (called PictureManagerPortType.aidl and PicturePortType.aidl) define the interfaces that declare the methods and fields available to a client. AIDL is a simple syntax that lets the designer declare an interface with one or more methods, that can take parameters and return values. These parameters and return values can be of any type, even other AIDL-generated interfaces. Then, the AIDL compiler creates an interface in the Java programming language from the AIDL interfaces. These interfaces have an inner abstract class named Stub that inherits the interface and implements a few additional methods necessary for the IPC call (Inter Procedure Call).

The next step is to create two classes that extend our previous interfaces PictureManagerPortType.Stub and PicturePortType.Stub and implements the methods we declared in our .aidl file. Then, we extend the Service class and override `Service.onBind(Intent)` to return an instance of one of our classes that implements one of our interfaces. The parameter intent plays the role of incoming message. The corresponding aidl descriptions of Figure 1 are given in Figure 5.

The primitive types are in direction by default. We limit the direction to what is truly needed, because marshalling parameters is time expensive. We have a class called `Picture` that we would like to send from a client process to the implementation process through an AIDL interface. We have made the Picture class which implements the Parcelable interface. The consequence is the overriding of the method public void `writeToParcel(Parcel out)` that takes the current state of the `Picture` and writes it to a parcel. The dual method is the method `public void readFromParcel (Parcel in)` that reads the value of a parcel into a `Picture`.

```
package fr.upec.lacl.project.gallery;

interface PictureManangerPortType {
    PicturePortType getPicture(long id);
    long putPicture(in Picture p);
    String getPictureDetail();
  // other methods are added in the case study.
}
```

```
package fr.upec.lacl.project.gallery;

// Declare Picture so AIDL can find it, knows
// that it implementsthe parcelable protocol.
parcelable Picture;
```

```
package fr.upec.lacl.project.gallery;

interface PicturePortType {
        Picture read();
        boolean update(long id, in Picture p);
        boolean available();
  // other methods are added in the case study.
}
```

Figure 5. aidl output files

B. REST services

The use of AIDL is required because of application sandboxing. Each application in Android runs in its own process. An application cannot directly access another application's memory space. In order to allow cross-application communication, Android provides the inter-process communication protocol. IPC protocols tend to get complicated because of all the marshaling/unmarshaling of data that is necessary, but it has also a main limit: it is not possible to use it in a remote manner.

Today, a remote access is a common requirement, but the installation of a Web server on a mobile platform is not so natural. Also, we propose to use remote access by the use of the REST (Representational State Transfer) service through the use of Google implementation called Restlet. It relies on a stateless, client-server, with cache communications protocol, and generally, in all cases, the HTTP protocol is used. REST is an architecture style for designing networked applications. The idea is that, rather than using complex mechanisms such as CORBA, RPC or SOAP to connect between machines, simple HTTP is used to make calls between machines.

As a programming approach, REST is a lightweight alternative to Web Services and RPC (Remote Procedure Calls) and Web Services (SOAP, WSDL, etc.). Much like Web Services, a REST service is platform-independent, language-independent, standards-based, runs on top of HTTP, and can easily be used in the presence of firewalls.

There are several reasons for having a Web server on a mobile phone. The main one is to allow third-party applications, on other phones or other platforms to access the phone remotely. This requires strong security mechanisms that are provided in part by the Restlet framework as well as network level authorizations by the carrier. We have decided to apply a Proxy design pattern to hide Restlet mechanism. So, each AIDL service is equipped with a Restlet service. To sum up, the AIDL implementation is used as a local facet on the mobile device and the Restlet implementation can be considered as a remote facet from other platforms.

In accordance with the Proxy design pattern, we have declared a subclass of the `ServerResource` class which belongs to the Restlet framework. Our class is called `PicturePortTypeResource` and has an attribute which is the previous AIDL implementation. Both classes implement the same business interface, but this last one provides our local service on the http protocol as a web resource. Figure 6 shows the main changes. Two technical packages are drawn to precisely the role of our technical classes.

Now, this mobile part is accessible from other mobile devices and also from workstation and application server, if necessary.

IV. CODE CONSTRUCTION

We design the embedded part with respect to such properties, such that the independence of the layers and interoperability remains. It means that the client part of the previous service does not know any technical details of our solution. This preserves the client from the changes of the new versions.

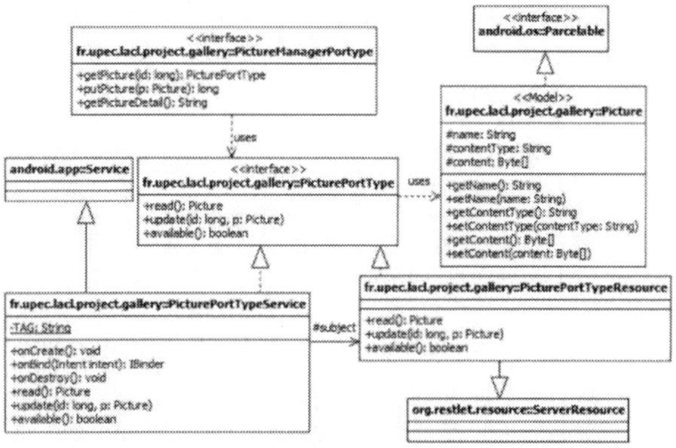

Figure 6. Design class diagram of the mobile part

A. *JavaEE implementation*

As explained previously, the middle layer is the pilot of the data collection. After the subscription of a mobile device, requests are sent periodically from the application server to the mobile device. Applications that model business work flows often rely on timed notifications. We schedule a timed notification to occur at time intervals. Then, the collected data are stored on the application server. Of course, other mobile devices can subscribe to that picture manager service even if several data collections are running. Both functionalities are isolated.

Another artifact is deployed on this application server: it is the inventory service. It is a stateless component which answers to the presentation layer running on a client workstation. The role of the inventory service is to answer to the client about the previous data collections. For instance, assume several mobile devices are previously registered, so a client can ask precisely to know where a picture, called "picture1" under a JPEG format is. The structure of that part is more convenient: it is a three tier layer. These different responsibilities of an application are broken up into distinct tiers, typically:

- The integration tier for data transformation and persistence services. The persistence unit is about the details which are collected during the data collection.
- The business tier for the validation, business rules, workflow and interfaces to external systems. The request is expressed by a subset of the features of the pictures. This means the content type, the size the annotations, etc.
- The presentation tier for user interface generation and lightweight validation. The web panels allow the requester to define his need.

The requests between the presentation and business layers are synchronous over TCP protocol, but a message broker is used to separate client and service. The exchanges are totally asynchronous between the business and the integration layers. This is essential because the integration part can be considered as a cache of the database for several Web applications.

B. *JavaSE implementation*

First, we use a web explorer to send http request and to display html tier. This display is a default graphical user interface used to send requests about the location of images. Next we have provided an API to develop new requests into programmatic clients. This is particularly useful for the automatic functional tests. This allows us to replace the use of Selenium tool of our own test application.

Our API also allows other developers to program new client tiers. It is based on the use of REST services which send requests to our business tier. Because we have chosen a REST implementation with the WADL generation (Web Application Description Language) [8], other developers can build their own version of our API. Also, SOAPUI tool [9] provides an easy way to create test suites of our business tier.

Our next case study is built with a lightweight client tier. In this context, the user is sure that the Web client is well suitable for the version of the business tier. Moreover, a comparison with other testing tools can be done, especially for performance measures.

V. CASE STUDY

As we explained in our contribution, our case study is about the management of the pictures on Smartphone. Several embedded devices are used, for instance, in a lab or in a classroom. So, a distributed tool is necessary to locate precisely where the pictures are. More generally, such kind of tool is useful for the whole management of the pictures. This means collect, remove, transfer, duplicate or transform to an appropriate format.

A. *Deployment view*

Before starting our case study, we have to deploy all artifacts on a given computer, as mentioned in Figure 2. Next, services have to be started by local servers. So, observations and measures could be done by a tester.

1) *Mobile data tier*

Under Android 4.2 operating system, the mobile devices are used by members of a laboratory to take photos. The camera records the pictures into a gallery where each of them corresponds to a separate file with a set of features (name, format, size, date, owner, etc.). Because, a gallery can be considered as a set of pictures, each picture has its own name for their identification. Often, the name is generated by the software component which manages the camera. This means that the name is not easily known by the scientist.

For a test phase, the first activity is to take several photos and then, register the mobile device as a data tier to a business server. This will engage a set of REST services as and points to the gallery of photos

2) *Business tier*

Its first objective is to be ready for receiving registration for all the mobile devices. From its point of view, the mobile devices are considered as a distributed data set of pictures. Concurrently, it performs a data collection about the features of the photos. This is not a collect of the photos because this will spend too much time. But this activity is to bind all the features, such as localization, into a registry for future requests. The inventory activity is managed by a timer. Also, regularly, a mobile device receives requests about new pictures if there are until the end of its registration onto the business server.

A third activity is to answer to the end users who want to localize the photos which are taken during a given period of time. Additional conditions can be set, such as the content type, the dimension of the picture, the size of the file, etc.

3) Client tier

In the test phase, we use a Web client for sending the requests. This client is received by sending an HTTP request from a navigator. It allows end users to define precisely the photos that they want to have access to. The answer of a request is a set of links. They can be used to access the embedded devices and the concrete photo. So, by the end of a test, this means: a request and a click on a hypertext link, a photo is displayed in the Web browser of the end user.

B. Artifact deployment

1) Mobile data tier

In order to install third party applications on our Android phone, we need to install APK (Android Package, files). The way we usually do is like the next iteration, but it is for testing:

- Plug in an USB cable to a PC and mount a SD card on my computer
- Get the APK file some
- where on the SD card on the phone
- Unmount the SD card on the PC, allowing the phone to see the SD card contents again
- Use Astro File Manager or some similar app to browse to that file on the SD card and select it, which will prompt us to answer if we want to install the app on the phone.

For the end users, we have defined a simpler strategy based on the use of the local repository. We deploy the .apk file on a local server (apache http server) with a static IP to make the file available for download. Now, the end user has to open the download link of the apk file in his mobile browser. The device will automatically start the installation after the download completes.

2) Business tier

We use an application server called JBoss where our applications are installed though an ear file (Enterprise Application aRchive). The standard configuration of JBoss provides a very simple and convenient system for deploying applications, but not necessarily suitable for a production environment.

As standard, the deploy directory is a configuration for deploying services, components and applications. Just include a file according to the specific type of component specifications for JBoss deployment take into account. It is possible to deploy the files to the deploy directory or its subdirectories. Each file type is taken into account by an appropriate service deployment. The EARDeployer service is used for our two main components: the registration of tablets and the data collector.

The AbstractWebDeployer service is used for the Web application called by the client. It is implemented for the servlet container TomcatDeployer. The archive files are in the format war (Web ARchive).

3) Client tier

In the test phase, we use a Web client for sending the requests. This is a set of JSP pages which belongs to the previous Web application. Also, the client tier is just a Web browser which is already installed on the computer of the client.

We also use Java Web Start, which is a mechanism for program delivery through a standard Web server. The Java GUI client is downloaded to the client and executed outside the Web browser. The GUI client does not need to be downloaded again in the next run. If the GUI client is updated, a new version will be downloaded automatically. The jar file contains an XML descriptor with an XML schema. It specifies the resources needed to run Java Web Start applications. It also defines the URL location of the jar file, VM arguments and other resources that JRE on the client side should know to start Java Web Start GUI client.

Such GUI client that needs access to system resources, like file system, network connections, etc., needs to be signed. Also, we generate a keystore (certificate) and attach it to the jar file. After that, an end user is able send requests to the business tier and also to access to mobile device.

C. Measures

Measuring the execution time is a really interesting, but also complicated topic. To do it right, in Java, we have to know a little bit about how the JVM works: generation decomposition and so on. But, we do not have the same VM on all the nodes of the network. The mobile devices have a DVM (Dalvik VM), the business tier and the client tier have a JVM (Java VM) but the versions are not correlated.

Also, we use a "ready to run" benchmarking framework that addresses many of our issues [7].

1) Measures Method execution time: The framework's essential class is named Benchmark. It is the only class that we use for the computation of measures; everything else is ancillary. Client and business tiers are observed by instances of the `Benchmark` class. We supply the code to be benchmarked to the `Benchmark` constructor. The benchmarking process is then fully automatic. Then, we generate a result report. The only restriction is that the code needs to be contained inside a `Callable` or `Runnable`. Otherwise, the target code can be anything expressible in the Java language.

2) Business tier Measures: there are two sets of measures. One is about the requests between the mobile devices and the application server. There two main tasks are: one is the registration of the mobile devices, and the second is the data collection which is started and ended by the application server.

The other set is about the treatment of the requests of the clients. Each request is received and treated by a business action which is also a `Runnable` instance. This means that we have measures on it. Both are interesting and their observations involve future improvements.

3) Results:

Table I presents measures of `RegistrationTask` class. It is a `Callable` subclass and its method is invoked when a mobile device needs to belong to the community of the mobile data tier. Next, a data collection will be applied.

TABLE I. REGISTRATION OF MOBILE DEVICES

Measures	Method execution time		
	First time	*Mean time*	*Standard deviation*
Registration	112.901 ms	108.501 ms	725.510 µs

In the meantime, we have additional information on it: deltas: -35.205 µs,+46.206 µs).

For the standard deviation execution time, we have the info: deltas: -161.405 µs, +361.108 µs

Table II presents measures of `DataCollectionTask` class. It is a `Runnable` subclass and its behavior is managed by a timer. At each interval of time, a data collection is started on a given mobile device. By the end, the changes are updated on the business server. This task is not linked to the previous one and several data collections are started concurrently in a manner that there is no effect from one data collection onto the other ones.

TABLE II. DATA COLLECTION ON A MOBILE DEVICE

Measures	Method execution time		
	First time	*Mean time*	*Standard deviation*
Data collection	225.910 ms	220.050 ms	555.004 µs

In the meantime, we have additional information on it: deltas: -31.520 µs,+41.602 µs).

For the standard deviation execution time, we have the info: deltas: -124.040 µs, +302.088 µs

Table III presents the measures of the `ClientRequest` class. It is also a `Runnable` subclass and its method is invoked when the end user sends a request about the URL addresses of several photos. Next, all the features of the user request are parsed and a result is computed from the previous data collections. Then, an answer is built with a set of URL instances. Each URL instance is a REST call to a service deployed on a mobile device.

TABLE III. CLIENT REQUEST ABOUT PHOTO ON DISTRIBUTED DEVICES

Measures	Method execution time		
	First time	*Mean time*	*Standard deviation*
Client request	164.621 ms	158.921 ms	605.233 µs

In the meantime, we have additional information on it: deltas: -41.115 µs,+51.261 µs).

For the standard deviation execution time, we have the info: deltas: -103.523 µs, +112.561 µs.

VI. ANALYSIS

The first time that `RegistrationTask` instance was called, it took 112.901 milliseconds to execute. A point estimate for the mean of the execution time is 108.501 milliseconds. The 95% confidence interval for the mean is about -35/+46 microseconds, which is relatively narrow, so the mean is known with confidence.

A point estimate for the standard deviation of the execution time is 725.510 microseconds. The 95% confidence interval for the standard deviation is about -161/+361 microseconds about the point estimate, namely [235.389, 1086.51] µs, which is relatively wide, so it is known with much less confidence. In fact, the warning at the end says that the standard deviation was not accurately measured. The result also warns about the outliers. They are not significant in this case because the scenarios contain network connections. This involves blockings and time consuming only for negotiation between mobile devices and business server.

In the case of the data collection the first time that `DataCollectionTask` instance was called, it took 225.910 milliseconds to execute. A point estimate for the mean of the execution time is 220.050 microseconds. The 95% confidence interval for the mean is approximately -31/+42 microseconds, which is relatively narrow too, so the mean is known with confidence.

The standard deviation of the execution time is 555.004 microseconds. The 95% confidence interval for the standard deviation is about -124/+302 microseconds about the point estimate, namely [430.964, 857.092] µs, which is less wide than the previous case. So it is known with much confidence. In fact, the warning at the end notes that the standard deviation comes from the size of data which is collected. The result also warns about the variability in the measurement. The latter is sometimes excluded from the data set.

The last case is about request treatment. The first time that `ClientRequest` instance, was called, it took 164.621 milliseconds to execute. A point estimate for the mean of the execution time is 158.921 microseconds. The 95% confidence interval for the mean is approximately -41/+51 microseconds, which is relatively narrow too, so the mean is known with confidence.

Then, the standard deviation of the execution time is 605.233 microseconds. The 95% confidence interval for the standard deviation is about -103/+112 microseconds about the point estimate, namely [501.71, 717.794] µs, which is relatively small. So, it is known with confidence. In fact, the warning at the end notes that the standard deviation comes from the number of requests which are received by the Web application. The result also indicates an experimental error because of the latency of the network. When we compute other measures on a sample with a bigger volume of requests, then this overhead time is hidden or recovered by the computation of the answers.

VII. Conclusion and Future Work

We have presented in this document our approach to the design (D), the implementation (I) and the evaluation (E) of mobile applications based on services. We have shown that there are two families of services: some of them are local and others are called from outside the mobile platform. Our esign is based on the use of UML diagrams and stereotypes to identify interfaces and the locality.

The implementation is based on Java programming and the use of frameworks, such as Restlet and Android. We have shown how to refine the diagrams towards a more technical description. A designer can sketch his/her applications with the use of local or remote services.

The evaluation is also described by interaction diagrams, which will become a test suite. We have built a case study based on our approach. It highlights all kinds of services (local and remote). So, interoperability is insured by the use of XML messages.

To conclude, our approach, called D.I.E. validates our design choice. Our experiments highlight the use of mobile devices as mobile data tier. As the number of embedded devices increases, our prototype shows that our software protocol supplies a way to exploit data on mobile devices without big data transfers.

References

[1] J. B., Warmer and A. G. Kleppe, "The object constraint language: Precise modeling with uml", addison-wesley object technology series, 1998.

[2] J. N. Herder, H. Bos, B. Gras, P. Homburg, and A. S. Tanenbaum, (2006, September). "Reorganizing UNIX for reliability", In Asia-Pacific Conference on Advances in Computer Systems Architecture (pp. 81-94). Springer Berlin Heidelberg.

[3] M. Gould, M. A. Bernabé, C. Granell, P. R. Muro-Medrano, J. Nogueras, C. Rebollo, and F. J. Zarazaga, (2002). "Reverse engineering SDI: Standards based Components for Prototyping", In *Proc. of the 8th European Comission GI&GIS Workshop, ESDI-A Work in Progress*.

[4] J. Kołodziej, S. U. Khan and E. G. Talbi, (2013). "Scalable optimization in grid, cloud, and intelligent network computing–foreword", Concurrency *and Computation: Practice and Experience, 25*(12), 1719-1721.

[5] T. Erl, (2004), "*Service-oriented architecture: a field guide to integrating XML and web services*", Prentice Hall PTR.

[6] O. Alliance, (2003). "*Osgi service platform, release 3",* IOS Press, Inc.

[7] O. M. G. Corba, "Common object request broker architecture" (Vol. 2), 1995.

[8] M. J. Hadley, (2006), "Web application description language (WADL)".

[9] C. Kankanamge, (2012), "*Web services testing with soapUI*", Packt Publishing Ltd.

[10] R. M. Soley and C. M. Stone, (1992), "*Object Management Architecture Guide: Revision 2.0"* (Vol. 92). Object Management Group.

BioWallet: A Biometric Digital Wallet

E. Benli, I. Engin, C. Giousouf, M. A. Ulak
Faculty of Computer and Informatics
Istanbul Technical University
34469, Maslak, Istanbul, Turkey
{benliel, engini, giousouf, ulak}@itu.edu.tr

Ş. Bahtiyar
Department of Computer Engineering
Boğaziçi University
34342, Bebek, Istanbul, Turkey
serif.bahtiyar@boun.edu.tr

Abstract— **People have used digital currencies to meet their online payment requirements in a more convenient, cheaper, and secure way. The currencies have been stored in digital wallets, where security is a significant challenge. In this paper, we propose a model that uses biometric methods to secure digital currencies within wallets. The proposed model improves both usability and security of payment transactions carried out with digital currencies, which are stored in wallets, by using fingerprints of users.**

Keywords- Digital currency; security; wallet; biometric.

I. INTRODUCTION

Recently, modern societies have become more connected than ever with the help of recent communication technologies. The connections have affected daily lives of people that have changed our habits. One of the most significant changes is our payment behavior, where payments shift from cash to digital money. This shift offers new benefits to corporations because the digital payment solutions have become more global. Therefore, the willingness to use such solutions has increased dramatically. Particularly, the research area of digital currencies has been given considerable attention. A digital currency is a currency that has neither physical representation nor belongs to a country. Nevertheless, it still has a value and allows individuals to make purchases or transactions with various amounts. For instance, the daily exchange of bitcoin may be $2 and $5 million USD. Recently, there are approximately $100 million bitcoins on the market [1].

The main issue about digital currencies is security. One of the significant challenges is the storage security of digital currencies that affects the anonymity of transactions. Existing storage systems have security vulnerabilities. This fact reduces the usability of digital currencies, which prevents the increase of online payment transactions. Some digital currency providers collaborate with third party security vendors to straighten the anonymity of transactions by enhancing security and trust. On the other hand, this approach does not provide complete trust since there is always a suspicion around what kind of security the third party provides related to the anonymity of transactions. This reduces trust in conventional digital currencies. Actually, some financial institutions use different security mechanisms to protect customers' data with the help of additional security mechanisms in the online environment, such as mobile and Web applications.

Wallets store digital currencies from where users obtain an address to use in order to make transactions. Simply, the sender must know the receiver's address in order to achieve a bitcoin transfer. Most of the time, third party organizations provide these addresses. Since the organizations can monitor transactions and they have all the critical information about users, anonymity and trust issues related to digital currency usage remain.

Most of the time, digital wallets are associated with specific hardware properties of computing devices to improve the security of the wallets for ensuring anonymity and trust. However, security usability is a challenge in those cases. For instance, if the device is lost, it is very hard or impossible to reach the coins within the wallet. Our motivation in this paper is the lack of usable security mechanisms that extend anonymity and trust for digital currencies. In this paper, we propose a conceptual model for securing credentials within digital wallets by using biometric methods. The model uses biometric sensors to reach biological properties of the users to increase usability. Particularly, we use data from fingerprint sensors to improve security usability of digital wallets for bitcoin like digital coins.

The reminder of the paper is organized as follows. Section II explains digital currencies and security. In Section III, we present our solution, BioWallet. Section IV is about the analysis of the proposed solution. Section V is devoted to conclusions and future works.

II. SECURITY AND DIGITAL CURRENCIES

There are various digital currencies, such as Bitcoin [1], Dogecoin [2], Mastercoin [2] and Litecoin [2]. Crypto currency is also used to refer to these currencies, since they have cryptographic properties. Bitcoin is a well-known and well-accepted digital currency. It is a distributed and open source digital currency system [1]. Bitcoin was designed by Satoshi Nakamoto in October, 2008. It addresses some crucial challenges, such as anonymity, double payment problem and illegal use of money. However, it does not provide a complete solution to these challenges [2][3]. Therefore, new digital currency systems similar to Zerocoin [1][4] have been developed.

Zerocoin [1], which was developed by Miers, solves some specific problems found in Bitcoin. It brings partial anonymity to transactions by hiding the senders' identity, but not the amount and the receivers' identity [4]. In addition, Zerocoin [1] tried to solve the double pay problem to ensure the integrity of digital currency systems. Although the structure of Zerocoin solves the double payment problem, it reduces the performance.

Ben et al. have introduced Zerocash [4] to solve the performance and anonymity problems of Zerocoin. They created DAP (Decentralized Anonymous Payment) scheme. Zerocash decreases the time of verification until 6 ms and hides the receiver identity by using DAP [4].

One of the most important parts of the digital currencies is wallets, since they allow users to store their bitcoins and transfer them whenever and wherever they desire. Although these wallets make the transaction process less challenging, they may be unprotected against thieves. For example, consider a user who is using a mobile bitcoin wallet to make his/her transactions. Someone can easily take that mobile device for a limited amount of time and send an amount of bitcoins to another bitcoin wallet account. The reason of this problem is the usage of traditional wallet systems that are working with just a password such as BlueWallet [9]. Therefore, it is obvious that a strong authentication mechanism is required for these wallet systems, especially for the people who desire to have it.

Hence, the biometric authentication systems are getting more common worldwide. Therefore many payment systems are shifting from traditional authentication methods to modern approaches like fingerprint, face recognition, ear recognition, and retina scan [6]. In personally identifiable authentication systems that contain critical data of the users, it is crucial to provide a strong access control mechanism to prevent unauthorized accesses to the confidential information related to financial information.

Bitcoin like cryptocurrencies still have security challenges. In 2011, intruders stole 25.000 bitcoins [1] that means we still have no strong access control for cryptocurrencies. On the other hand, Zerocoin has attempted to solve the double pay problem, which is one of the most essential challenges. In order to solve this problem, bigger sized spend proofs are used. As the block chain keeps the spend proofs, it may result in deployment problems [7]. In order to maintain the anonymity, Zerocoin uses zero-knowledge proof [7].

The protection of wallets where users keep their digital properties, such addresses and keys, is a significant challenge. Password based authentication methods are the common way to protect current digital wallets. On the other hand, passwords are prone to many attacks or simply they may be stolen. For instance, someone may make coin transactions from these wallets by taking possession of the passwords or device of the user.

Recent researches show that to get secret keys and passwords from a mobile device is a very easy process. Researchers have accomplished this using an ordinary magnetic probe to get the private key of some wallet applications [8]. This shows how vulnerable existing digital wallets are. One of the best ways to avoid this kind of problems is using biometric authentication methods, such as fingerprint and retina scan. [9].

BioWallet offers a new method for the specified problem. Bitcoin users can protect their information on storage by using the fingerprint based access control of BioWallet. Specifically, users need to enroll their fingerprints for the initial installation of the wallet. Moreover, a user must verify her fingerprint in every transaction. BioWallet improves the security of Zerocash that offers pure anonymity. We believe that the proposed solution extends the security of digital currency systems, particularly for crypto currencies.

III. BioWallet

One of the most useful methods to authenticate users is to use their biometric information. Almost all systems allow users to use their biometric information in terms of hardware. Additionally, the security of biometric methods is a proven fact [10][11][12].

In our model, users initially register their biometric credentials to the system. The information gathered from users is encrypted with 1024 or 2048-bits RSA (Rivest, Shamir, Adleman) keys and it is kept in server in order to protect the data. Figure 1 shows our model about secure registration process using fingerprint.

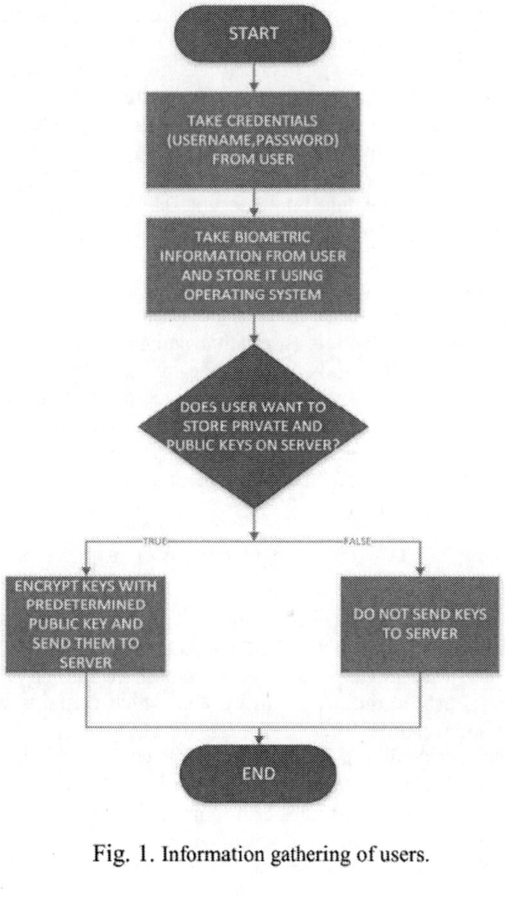

Fig. 1. Information gathering of users.

Below are the abbreviations we used in the encryption process.

PR_U : *Private key of user*
PU_U : *Public key of user*
PR_S : *Private key used in server*
PU_S : *Public key used in server*
$E(data, key)$: *Encryption of data with given key*
$D(cipher, key)$: *Decryption of cipher with given key*
$ciper = E(PR_U, PU_S)$
$PR_U = D(cipher, PR_S)$

After registration, in order to allow users to send bitcoins, we have two approaches. In the first approach, a user is authorized for a predetermined time (i.e. 10 minutes). In this manner, users are allowed to accomplish multiple transactions without approving their identities. However, it may be vulnerable against some attacks.

In the second approach, a user provides its identity for each transaction she initiates. This makes it harder for an attacker to steal coins. Figure 2 explains the flow of this approach. Here, we use two-phase authorization system in the model. In this way, we eliminate potential vulnerabilities emerged from using only biometric information.

During the process of sending bitcoins, a standard public key encryption is used. However, if a user loses his/her credentials (i.e. losing phone or logging out from the application), then he/she also loses the related keys.

When the user registers onto the system, a public-private keys pair is created. Then, the keys are sent to the server after encrypting them with a predetermined public key. The private key that is used to decrypt the encrypted public-private keys of user are kept on the server. Therefore, no one is able to reach the keys of the user.

A user may lose his/her device and he/she obtains a new device, where the user installs the wallet. When the user gives his/her credentials (username and password) and the answer of the security question, the system creates a new private and public key for the user. Since the server has the old encrypted version of private-public keys of the user and the private key to decrypt them, the system automatically sends the bitcoins left in the old account of the user to the new created account.

IV. ANALYSIS OF BIOWALLET

We compare BioWallet with existing wallets to show the advantages of the proposed solution. The first wallet system that we compare with BioWallet is BlueWallet. BlueWallet is a hardware device that uses Bluetooth technology. The device is a little mobile hardware box which contains input and output screens [9].

The most similar product is Case which is a bitcoin wallet that offers complete security in a hardware component that allows to spend or transfer bitcoins [13]. They claim that they do not save users' fingerprints directly in their database, but rather that the fingerprint patterns are stored and that helps to authenticate a user. The main lack of the product may be that it does not give chance to its users to reacquire their money when the users somehow lose them. Besides, Case uses a piece of hardware for performing all bitcoin operations. On the other hand, BioWallet uses a device built-in fingerprint scanner to scan fingerprints and keeps them on operating system. Therefore, it does not need any additional hardware but the smart phone that supports fingerprint scan.

There are many digital wallet systems, which store Bitcoin like cryptocurrencies by using only software solutions on Android or iOS. These options ensure diverse usage of personal smartphones as a digital wallet. The biggest advantage of mobile application wallets against any other wallet types is the availability when a user needs it. On the other hand, if there is no screen lock or another protection mechanism on smartphones, thieves can steal the smartphone and access any critical information. For example, one of the well-known wallet applications is Bitcoin Wallet. Although Bitcoin Wallet has some useful features like QR Code (Quick Response Code) scanning and more than one bitcoin receive address support, it does not have any security barrier against reaching the application except a single password.

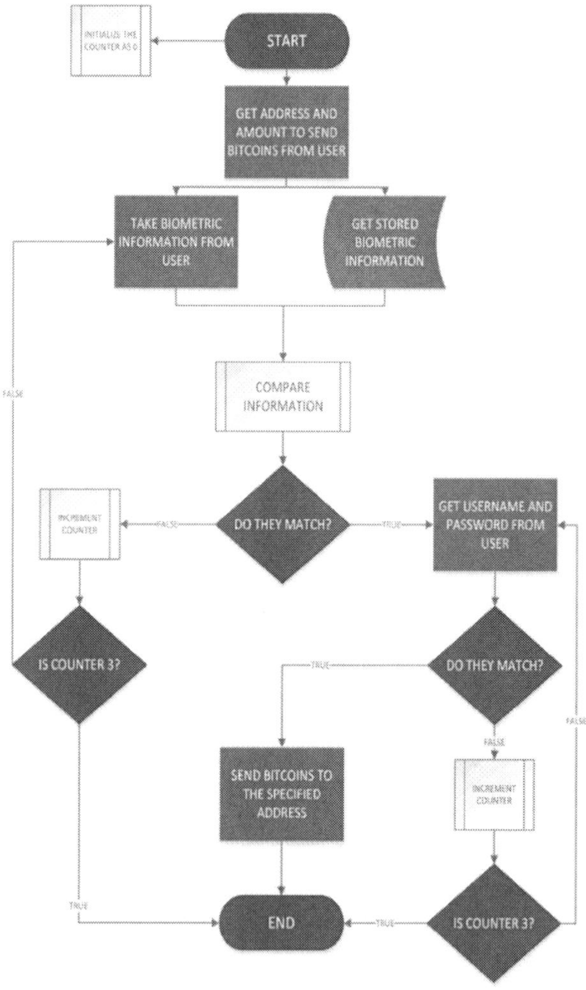

Fig. 2. Two phase authentication system

BioWallet protects the digital assets and transaction process with two-phase authentication system that employs fingerprint and password authentication. Additionally, BioWallet does not store any fingerprint data online to be able to preserve privacy. All personal data are stored locally. Based on the personal needs of a user, private and public keys can be stored at the cloud server in an encrypted way except fingerprint data. When users need to use a new device, the system sends user's money to the new device. Thus, digital wallet users can continue to use their digital money from the new device.

There is another kind of wallet for performing digital currency activities. It is called Web wallets where users can directly reach it from Web browser. Ordinary Bitcoin clients require at least 14 GB disk capacity and they need many hours to complete synchronization with block chain. Owing to Web wallets, no need for these requirements anymore. However, this kind of wallets are vulnerable from the server side. For example, 923 BTCs (Bitcoin) were stolen from OzCoin system [14].

TABLE I.
SUMMARY COMPARISON OF BIOWALLET AND OTHER WALLETS

Wallet Name	**Fingerprint Authentication**	**Mobile Support**	**Basic Wallet Operations**	**Easy Transfer**	**Software Solution**
BioWallet	✓	✓	✓	✓	✓
BlueWallet	×	✓	✓	✓	×
Case	✓	✓	✓	✓	×
Bitcoin Wallet	×	✓	✓	✓	✓
Web Wallets	×	×	✓	✓	✓
Desktop Wallets	×	×	✓	✓	✓

The last type of bitcoin wallets is desktop wallets. Desktop computers are safer than mobile computers or systems against physical theft. Moreover, almost all desktop computer systems have a system password at the beginning. Thus, fingerprint protection is not really solving security issues on personal computers when compared with the smartphones. That's why BioWallet is primarily created for mobile platform users. We compare BioWallet and other wallets in Table I.

V. CONCLUSION AND FUTURE WORK

Password based authentication mechanisms are inadequate for the protection of currencies within digital wallets. In this paper, we propose a solution that uses biometric methods to secure coins within digital wallets. A user can easily guard her digital coins by using BioWallet with her fingerprints that will extend the usability of digital currency.

As a future work, we will implement BioWallet. Moreover, we have been working to integrate other biometric methods to BioWallet, such as retina and face recognitions.

ACKNOWLEDGMENT

This work is supported by the Turkish State Planning Organization (DPT) under the TAM Project, number 2007K120610.

REFERENCES

[1] I. Miers, C. Garman, M. Green, and A. D. Rubin, "Zerocoin: Anonymous Distributed E-Cash from Bitcoin," in 2013 IEEE Symposium on Security and Privacy (SP), 2013, pp. 397–411.

[2] F. Tschorsch and B. Scheuermann, "Bitcoin and Beyond: A Technical Survey on Decentralized Digital Currencies," in *IEEE Communications Surveys & Tutorials*, vol. 18, no. 3, pp. 2084-2123, third quarter 2016.

[3] S. Barber, X. Boyen, E. Shi, and E. Uzun, "Bitter to Better — How to Make Bitcoin a Better Currency," in Financial Cryptography and Data Security, A. D. Keromytis, Ed. Springer Berlin Heidelberg, 2012, pp. 399–414.

[4] E. Ben-Sasson et al., "Zerocash: Decentralized Anonymous Payments from Bitcoin," 349, 2014.

[5] http://www.coindesk.com/data/bitcoin-daily-transactions/. [Accessed: 18-Nov-2016].

[6] N. L. Clarke and S. M. Furnell, "Authentication of users on mobile telephones – A survey of attitudes and practices," Computers & Security, vol. 24, no. 7, pp. 519–527, Oct. 2005.

[7] C. Garman, M. Green, I. Miers, and A. D. Rubin, "Rational Zero: Economic Security for Zerocoin with Everlasting Anonymity," in Financial Cryptography and Data Security, R. Böhme, M. Brenner, T. Moore, and M. Smith, Eds. Springer Berlin Heidelberg, 2014, pp. 140–155

[8] D. Genkin, L. Pachmanov, I. Pipman, E. Tromer, and Y. Yarom, "ECDSA Key Extraction from Mobile Devices via Nonintrusive Physical Side Channels," in *Proceedings of the 2016 ACM SIGSAC Conference on Computer and Communications Security*, New York, NY, USA, 2016, pp. 1626–1638.

[9] T. Bamert, C. Decker, R. Wattenhofer, and S. Welten, "BlueWallet: The Secure Bitcoin Wallet," in Security and Trust Management, S. Mauw and C. D. Jensen, Eds. Springer International Publishing, 2014, pp. 65–80.

[10] V. Matyás Jr. and Z. Ríha, "Biometric Authentication - Security and Usability," in Proceedings of the IFIP TC6/TC11 Sixth Joint Working Conference on Communications and Multimedia Security: Advanced Communications and Multimedia Security, Deventer, Netherlands, 2002, pp. 227–239.

[11] "Android 6.0 APIs | Android Developers." [Online]. Available: https://developer.android.com/about/versions/marshmallow/android-6.0.html. [Accessed: 12-Nov-2016].

[12] "RSA Laboratories - Has the RSA algorithm been compromised as a result of Bernstein's Paper?" [Online]. Available: http://www.emc.com/emc-plus/rsa-labs/historical/has-the-rsa-algorithm-been-compromised.htm. [Accessed: 19-Nov-2016].

[13] "Case - The world's most secure and easy-to-use bitcoin wallet." [Online]. Available: https://choosecase.com/faq.html. [Accessed: 18-Nov-2016].

[14] A. Gervais, G. O. Karame, V. Capkun, and S. Capkun, "Is Bitcoin a Decentralized Currency?," *IEEE Security Privacy*, vol. 12, no. 3, pp. 54–60, May 2014

Security of Mobile Agents in Distributed Java Agent Development Framework (JADE) Platforms

Timo Bayer and Christoph Reich
University of Applied Science Furtwangen, Germany
Email: {timo.bayer, christoph.reich}@hs-furtwangen.de

***Abstract*—Mobile Software Agent has become increasingly interesting as a basic software technology in the field of Internet of Things, like Smart Cities, Smart Home, Industry 4.0, etc. since it offers dynamic adaption, autonomous actions, flexible maintenance, parallel processing, and is tolerant to network faults. In particular, it is very challenging to guarantee security because of characteristic features such as mobility and autonomy. This paper addresses specific security requirements for mobile software agents and possible threats for agent system operations in the context of Java Agent Development Framework (JADE) platform. The main objective of the paper is to show existing vulnerabilities and security gaps by analyzing the security of agent platform JADE, showing existing improvements of the confidentiality of software agents merging from one agent platform to another and introducing trusted agents and their implementation in JADE.**

***Keywords*-JADE security; mobile agent security; agent migration; agent confidentiality; agent trust**

I. Introduction

One of the big challenges for the design and the use of Multi-Agent Systems (MASs) is the complexity caused by their dynamic, autonomy, and high decentralization nature. MASs are often operated in different networks, that belong to various organizations, and consist of components with different responsibilities (Section III). Consequentially, there is a wide range of attack vectors and a number of difficulties arise during the integration of appropriate protective measures. A particular challenge is the transfer of software agents, which can merge from one platform to the other. Obviously it is necessary to ensure a secure migration of the mobile agents and to protect the underlying agent system against potential malicious agents. The agents may operate in different MAS platform providers. In order to protect the agent owner and the receiver platform, it has to be ensured their integrity and adequate trust level during the migration process. A multi provider distributed MAS approach for auditing data access policies between multiple hybrid cloud environments, for instance, has been proposed in Ruebsamen et.al [1]. There, for example, agents migrate from platform to platform to verify the compliance of correct data access along the provider chain. The objectives of the paper are to show existing vulnerabilities and security gaps by analyzing the existing security implementations of agent platform JADE, show existing improvements of the confidentiality of software agents merging from one agent platform to another and introducing trusted agents and their implementation in JADE. The paper is structured as follows: In Section II we presents the related work. In Section III-A, we discuss the requirement for multi-agent systems to have a security evaluation while considering the characteristics of mobile agents. This paper focuses on Java Agent Development Framework (JADE), its existing security implementations Jade Security (Section III-B), a security analysis with regard to the specific requirements of mobile agents, and to point out the security gaps of JADE (see Section III-C). Finally, additional security measures, especially in the field of confidentiality and trust are discussed and adapted for an appropriate use in the context of JADE in Section III-D and Section IV. Section V concludes the paper.

II. Related Work

A detailed discussion about agent technology, particularly with reference to the specific features, technical characteristics, possible applications and the arising potential of this technology can be found in [2]-[3]. To increase the field of application, big efforts have been made in designing and developing suitable security measures.

Ahila et al. reported in [4] about the security requirements for mobile agent systems and pointed out some existing security threats as well as general security enhancements. Particularly, security concepts protecting the confidentiality of mobile agents have been introduced. In this paper, some of the illustrated security concepts are being adapted to the applications of the framework JADE.

Bürkle et al. described in [5] existing security implementations in agent framework JADE and pointed out some vulnerabilities allowing attacks to reduce the availability of agents or the agent system by using targeted denial of service attacks. Furthermore, they pointed out some limitations in the security implementations of the agent framework JADE, including some restrictions on the permission model for mobile agents. The described vulnerabilities conform with the results shown in this work.

Vila et al. also evaluated in [6] the existing security implementations of JADE and reported some additional ameliorations concerning security, being adopted to a concrete application scenario. The analysis focussed on encrypting the communication between agents and on ensuring the availability of the agent system.

Piette et al. described in [7] the use of mobile agent systems for configuration, deployment, and monitoring of distributed applications in the domain of Ambient Intelligence. They focus on the ability to enhance privacy by hiding information using the agent architecture. Such a scenario includes sensitive information and therefore requires the capacity to protect the agent system. The shown scenario clarifies the necessity to consider the particular security requirements of mobile agents.

Geetha and Jayakumar evaluated in [8], the general security requirements for mobile agent systems and existing security measures. Especially, they pointed out some weaknesses in the field of protecting the carried data of mobile agents. To mitigate this issue, they implemented a trust and reputation management to provide a secure path for mobile agent data protection. This work is similar to the approach presented in Section IV, but focused more on the data carried by the agent rather than their general trustability.

Dong et al. [9] argue that due to the open nature of communication channels in networked multi-agent systems, the network is vulnerable to various malicious cyber attacks. A specific edge-bound content modification cyber attack has been designed which compromises and destabilizes the multi-agent systems. The paper describes attack detection schemes and it proposes an attack mitigation scheme. Such an approach can also be used to enhance the general security threats shown in Section III-C.

Gengarajoo et al. introduced in [10] an approach to ensure trust of cooperating agents. The proposed trust evaluation model determins the trust of an agent, based on experience gained from interaction among agents. In addition to our approach presented in Section IV, it relies on further runtime information. Therefore, the two approaches can be combined to ensure trust among the whole agent life-cycle.

III. Security in Multi-Agent Systems

Multi-Agent Systems (MASs) provide an environment for multiple interacting intelligent agents, that cooperate to solve problems. There are several key characteristics, such as adaptation, scalability, autonomy, communication between agents, etc. (see [4]). Frameworks, like JADE [11], exist to support the agent system development, operation, and maintenance. Next to the MASs characteristics, JADE also supports, mobile agents, which merge from one platform to the other. Mobile agents, as stated in Gitter et al. [12], are autonomous software components, being able to change their execution environment in heterogeneous networks to perform predefined tasks in the name of its user [12]. Besides the general security requirements of agent technology, an extensive security analysis has to be done taking into account the typical MAS's features. In this section, we first determine the security requirements of a MAS (Section III-A), then introduce existing security implementations of JADE (Section III-B) and finally, compare them to determine the remaining security gaps (Section III-C).

A. Security requirements for mobile agents

To determine the MAS security requirements, it has to be considered: a) the agent specific security issues, like data access restriction, agent data protection, etc. b) the security protection of the platform and execution environment and c) the general security requirements, like ensuring the integrity, confidentiality and availability of the agent system. This includes security measures of agent specific access control, resource management usage, and the platform protection against malicious agents arriving from other locations. The following lists the security requirements of multi-agent systems. The bold text indicates threads listed in Fig. 1:

Network Security: Network security is essential to ensure the agent's integrity and confidentiality on transmission level. Existing security solutions like secure sockets or correspondingly configured firewalls may be used to guarantee a secure transmission between the system components and protect the system against **Denial of Service** attacks [13].

Confidentiality of Mobile Agents: The ability to change the execution environment autonomously, requires appropriate solutions to ensure the confidentiality of mobile agents. For many applications, a standard point-to-point encryption provides adequate protection against **eavesdropping the communication** and **injecting messages**. But there exist more complex applications requiring the consideration of additional security measures. Agents often collect and process information on different network locations. In case an agent migrates into multiple platforms in various areas of trust only selected platforms should be authorized to access the information collected by the agent. Therefore, a platform specific encryption is necessary to protect the agent against **unauthorized access to collected data**.

Integrity of Mobile Agents: An illegal **manipulation of mobile agents** may take place on transport level or triggered by destructive system components or malicious remote agent platforms on the migration path. Particular attention is also necessary to protect the agent against destructive platforms may attacking the availability of mobile agents (**agent paralyzation**). After the agent reaches its destination platform, the platform executes the agent actions. Thus, the agent is entirely managed and operated by the underlying platform. Consequently, a malicious agent platform is able to manipulate the agent. This risk leads to an additional security requirement, comprising the agent protection against unauthorized manipulations during the migration process, respectively to find a way to detect such a manipulation.

Malicious Agent Protection: The ability to change the execution environment autonomously not only results in higher agent security requirements but also requires an additional consideration of the agent platform protection against

unauthorized resource access and **platform paralyzation**. One additional security requirement in the context of agent platform protection is to be able to comprehend the whole migration path of a mobile agent accessing the platform. The migration of a mobile agent may be triggered by several different components and therefore the agent platform is not able to follow the migration path precisely. The information on which platforms an agent was executed previously is helpful to determine the general trust of an incoming agent and its memorized data. Therefore, the ability to follow the migration path is an essential security requirement to protect the platform against malicious agents.
Trust Level of Merged Agents: The execution of a mobile agent on a remote platform represents a code injection because an unknown program code which is only partly controllable by the platform will be executed. The question is: "Can the agent be trusted?" To answer this question we need a metric to verify the trust level of an incoming agent. At present, this is not possible. There is a risk that malicious agents perform actions that will cause severe damage to the underlying platform (**inject malicious agents**). For example, DoS attacks against the availability of services, extraction of confidential information, etc. Therefore, it is necessary to be able to verify the trust level of the incoming agent before it is accepted. Otherwise, the platform has to prevent the execution of actions by the agent.

B. *Security implementations in JADE*

The basic version of JADE provides no specific security implementations to protect the agent system. Nevertheless, to achieve a basic security level, the framework has to be extended with security plugins provided by the JADE manufacturer. The plugin design allows flexibility and the ability to include only the necessary plugins, which are needed for the application-specific security level.

The most important security expansion, providing the basic security measures, is called *JADE Security* [14]. The *JADE Security* extension is based on the *Java Security Model* and consists of several security implementations, including the authentication of system components, the corresponding permission allocation, as well as message encryption and digital signature service [14]. To provide these security measures, the containers and agents have to be configured with additional information, including certificates and permission stores. As the signature and encryption service only secure the transmitted messages but not the agent transfer, additional security plugins like JADE Public Key Infrastruktur (*JADE-PKI*) [15] and Instant Message Transfer Protocol (IMTP) over Secure Sockets Layer (SSL) (*IMTPoverSSL*) [16] are necessary providing an encoded communication channel between the containers. Further information concerning available security measures is to be found in [5][6][14].

C. *Missing Security in JADE*

Assuming the use of the previous described security expansions, it is possible to reduce some general security threats. This includes the **eavesdropping of the communication**, the **injection of messages, agent and platform paralyzation**, and the **unauthorized access to resources** of the platform. Nevertheless, some security aspects were left unconsidered. Figure 1 shows an overview of existing security threats as well as the respective security implementations of agent platform JADE.

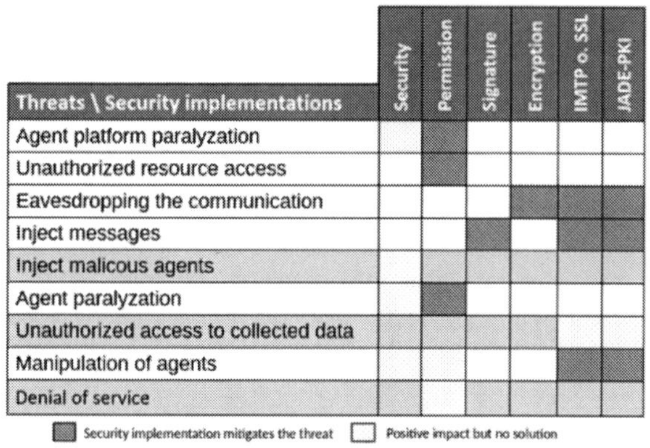

Figure 1. Security threats and their respective security implementations

Here, we focus on the "yellow" and "grey" marked boxes, which show the missing JADE implementations.

Agent and Platform Paralyzation: The agents and platforms have to be protected against misbehaviour like overloading agents with spam messages caused by faulty or malicious system components. To be able to reduce this threat extensive permission restrictions are necessary.

Unauthorized Access to Collected Data & Manipulation of Agents: Another security issue is the lack of protection against **unauthorized access to collected data**. This issue needs to be discussed with reference to two different aspects. First, the unauthorized access to mobile agent's information during the transmission process and secondly the information access by unauthorized agent platforms. In case one of the expansions *JADE-PKI* or *IMTPoverSSL* is used it is possible to ensure the agent's confidentiality during the transmission process and also avoid illegal **manipulation of agents**. However, the access by unauthorized agent platforms is far more complicated. Due to the fact that the security expansion does not have an authorization model that fits for the mobile agent's needs, and therefore no location based access rights can be granted, the expansion does not offer a sufficient protection [5]. Therefore, additional security mechanisms are required protecting the agent's confidential data, specific to its current execution environment.

Injecting Malicious Agents: The available security extensions focus on the operations of static agent systems. The specific security requirements for the agent mobility [14] is not covered sufficiently. There are no effective mechanisms available to verify that a mobile agent is not malicious but trustable, before an agent is accepted and actions processed on the destination platform. A minimum protection is already guaranteed by the provided authentication of particular components, but this only applies to the agent platforms and containers. No platform-specific authentication model is available for mobile agents. As soon as a container or agent platform is authenticated in the system, it is allowed to migrate all its containing agents to a remote execution environment. After the migration of the agents to the destination component, the trust of incoming agents cannot be verified any more. Depending on the application scenario the worst security issues, including **unauthorized resource access** and the execution of a malicious program code (**injecting malicious agents**) causing severe damage to the remote computer system, may result from this security restriction.

Denial of Service (DoS): A general security issue is the **Denial of Service (DoS)** attacks. Although it is already possible to mitigate the impact of DoS attacks, by a targeted restriction of the communication, specific characteristics of DoS attacks will remain a threat. These attacks often take advantage of specific vulnerabilities of the implementation or specific features of the agent framework. Relating to JADE, this usually includes the recursive cloning of agents, the overloading of agents via spam messages as well as tailored restrictions on the availability of the *Agent Management System (AMS)* component [5]. By means of a strong limitation of the component's privileges and the use of appropriate communication rules, it is possible to mitigate the impact of these attacks.

The described vulnerabilities refer mostly to agent systems comprising several areas of trust and use the ability to migrate agents to remote locations. For static agent systems an appropriate security level is reached by the existing security expansion. The following sections introduce some additional security measures to protect the system against the uncovered threats.

D. Confidentiality of Mobile Agent Data

Mobile agents often migrate across multiple platforms and collect sensitive data at each site. In order to be able to protect the collected information, additional security measures are necessary to restrict the data access to selected platforms. One approach to achieve this protection is the use of an environmental key generation as described in [4].

The primary objective of the environmental key generation scenario is to hide the data collected by the agent until a particular environmental condition is reached on the destination platform. A possible environmental condition could be, for example, to find a certain environmental key or the availability of predefined resources or the existence of cooperating agents. The described security objective is of particular importance in case an agent has to cross multiple platforms to perform its predefined task. In such a scenario, the platforms should only be able to access selected information. The sensitive information is encrypted by using a key being partly known by the agent and the information only may be decrypted by the agent itself. After the agent reaches the destination platform, the predefined environmental condition is checked. When the condition is met, an activation key is generated to decrypt the enciphered information carried by the agent. To generate the activation key the part of the key known by the agent will be combined with the condition matching result. Therefore, without meeting the environmental condition, neither the agent nor the executing platform are able to decrypt the information.

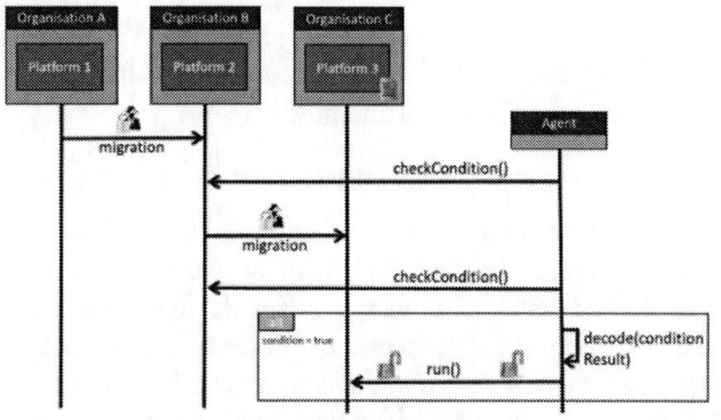

Figure 2. Environmental key generation scenario

Figure 2 shows three agent platforms being operated by different organizations. In Figure 2, the environmental condition is met when a platform contains a configuration file with a certain configuration entry, such as the use of appropriate encryption channels like HTTP for web servers. As soon as the first platform is reached, the encrypted agent starts to search for the condition matching file. In case the current platform does not meet the condition, the agent is not able to decrypt the carried information and therefore the platform is not able to access the data. Nevertheless, the agent is able to perform all kinds of tasks at its current location except the use of the encrypted information. After another migration takes place, the agent reaches the final destination. There, the agent will find the specified configuration file and finally decrypt the carried information by using the already partly known key in combination with a predefined entry in the configuration file. Thus, the agent as well as the executing platform are able to access the information.

To implement the described security measure, the agents have to be able to encrypt and decrypt specific data parts and to check the environmental condition. The security measure has been integrated into the agent framework JADE without the necessity to deploy customized execution environments. Besides the described environmental key generation, additional security measures exist to enhance the confidentiality of mobile agents. An algorithm for the generation of an encrypted function (see [13]) is implemented into the basic platform of the agent. The encrypted function is integrated into the agent after the agent has been instantiated. After the agent reaches its destination platform, the function may be executed by using location-specific arguments. The platforms of the agent's migration path will be able to execute the agent but no further information about the implemented functionality or the containing data is accessible. In case a platform comprises the required key to decrypt the function, the platform is able to access the information.

The security measures mentioned provide an extensive confidentiality protection for mobile agents. However, this kind of mechanisms may lead to a considerable danger with reference to the security of the agent platforms. The platforms have to execute an incoming agent without any additional information about its level of trust. The following section introduces some solutions to provide the ability to check the level of trust of incoming agents.

IV. Trustworthy Mobile Agents

In order to achieve a comprehensive protection of the agent system, appropriate security measures to verify the overall trust level of a merging mobile agent have to be realized. A minimal protection is already provided by the use of encrypted and signed communication between the different locations. A signed communication only ensures the integrity and the origin of an arriving agent but does not provide the ability to make assumptions about the general trust level, additional security considerations are necessary.

There are two possibilities to increase the trust level of an mobile agent: a) Registering verified agents at a trusted authority repository (third party) described in more detail in this section. b) Tracking of the migration path. This mainly comprises recording of previously passed locations of the agent and therefore helps to achieve the traceability to other system components (see [17]).

A. Repository of Trustworthy Agents

One way to mitigate is to enhance the agent system with a trusted authority, comprising the verified and considered trustworthy agents. Before the agents are stored in the trusted authority, the authority analyzes the program code by examining the defined behaviour. When an agent is entering a new platform, the platform is in a position to check whether the agent store contains the agent, using the unique identifier. If the trusted authority comprises the incoming agent, additional information about the agent may be checked. Such information may include information about the defined behaviour as well as the corresponding hash value. Further analysis, based on the behaviour, the requested hash value may be used to verify whether the incoming agent matches with the expected and authorized agent. In case the incoming agent is not to be found in the agent store or the hash values are different, the agent may be rejected by the platform. Figure 3 visualizes the architecture and shows a high-level process overview.

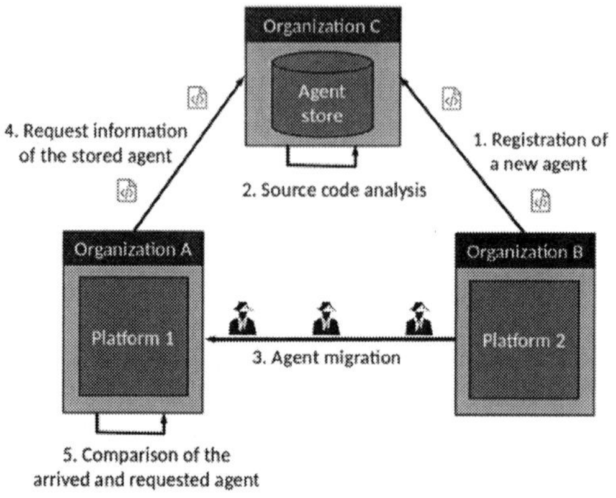

Figure 3. Overview: Repository of Trustworthy Agents

A challenge with reference to the hash-based check of identity is to generate comparable hash values. This challenge primarily originates from the fact that agent platforms append additional information to the agents during the instantiation time. For example, this includes the agent identifier and some information about the current execution environment. The local information leads to different hash values, depending on the current location. Another problem is that the involved components have different data formats representing the same agent.

The trusted authority's data format is the program code to verify the agent's behaviour, whereas the platform's data format, representing the migrated agent, is an instance of the class *Agent*. Nevertheless, to generate meaningful and comparable hash values, the values have to be created at class level instead of instance level. This kind of hash values guarantees that the incoming agent's behaviour matches with the stored and verified program code. Information about the current execution status as well as the collected data at runtime were left unconsidered in this approach.

B. Integration of Repository into JADE

JADE provides a function *serve(HorizontalCommand cmd)*, being activated automatically when a new agent reaches the platform. In order to be able to use the described security measure, this function has to be expanded by an additional application logic. Figure 4 shows the process flow when the expanded function *serve(..)* is executed.

After de-serializing the agent, after it has reached the platform, the agent's unique identifier is extracted by the *getAID()* function defined by the superclass *Agent*. The identifier is used to check whether the trusted authority is able to identify the requested agent. In case the agent is known by the agent store, the trusted authority responses with the corresponding hash value. Afterwards, the platform

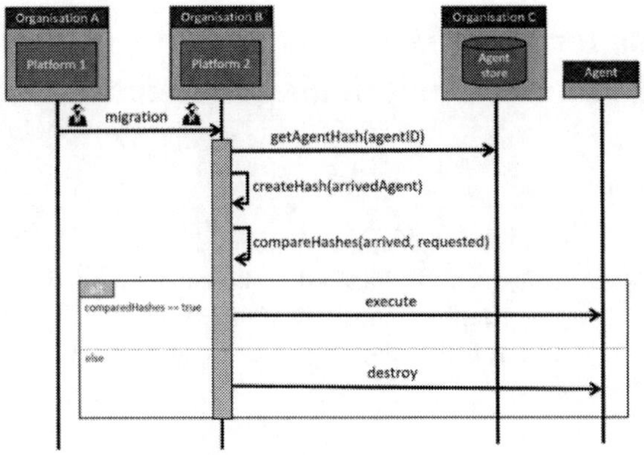

Figure 4. Process flow of extended serve(..) function

generates a hash value for the incoming agent, which subsequently is compared with the requested value. Assuming that the result of the comparison is positive the default implementation of the *serve(..)* function will be continued and the agent is accepted. In case the requested agent will not be found in the trusted authority or the compared hash values diverge, the incoming agent will be rejected and the platform prevents its execution.

If the described security measure is applied, the agent system provides the ability to restrict the authorized agents previously and thus the system is protected against malicious agents. The potential arises especially in large systems consisting of several independent organizations. By means of the use of the agent store a situation of mutual trust between the different organizations may be created. A proof of concept implementation can be found in [18].

V. CONCLUSION

The existing security expansions (JADE Security [14]) for JADE already reduces some of the general security threats. Reflecting on the specific security requirements for mobile agents, it will be realized that some security issues remain unconsidered. This paper gives a summary of some possible security measures, the missing security measures by JADE, and describes how to achieve the confidentiality of mobile agent data and how to protect the platform against malicious agents. However, further efforts are necessary to achieve an extensive security level for the whole agent system. A future work will be to develop easily integrable security plugins to increase the practicability of the described solutions.

REFERENCES

[1] T. Ruebsamen and C. Reich, "Supporting cloud accountability by collecting evidence using audit agents," in 2013 IEEE 5th International Conference on Cloud Computing Technology and Science, vol. 1, 2013, pp. 185–190.

[2] Y. S. . K. Leyton-Brown, Multiagent Systems: Algorithmic, Game-Theoretic, and Logical Foundations. Cambridge University Press, 2009, ISBN: 978-0521899437.

[3] G. Jezic, Y.-H. J. Chen-Burger, R. J. Howlett, and L. C. Jain, Eds., Agent and Multi-Agent Systems: Technology and Applications. Springer International Publishing, 2016, ISBN: 9783319398822.

[4] S. Ahila and K. Shunmuganathan, "Overview of mobile agent security issues - solutions," in Information Communication and Embedded Systems. Institute of Electrical and Electronics Engineers, 2014, pp. 1–6, ISBN: 9781479936984.

[5] A. Bürkle, A. Hertel, W. Müller, and M. Wieser, "Evaluating the security of mobile agent platforms," Autonomous Agents and Multi-Agent Systems, vol. 18, no. 2, 2009, pp. 295–311, ISSN: 1387-2532.

[6] A. R. X. Villa, A. Schuster, "Security for a multi-agent system based on jade," Computers & Security, vol. 26, 2007, pp. 391 – 400.

[7] F. Piette, C. Caval, A. El Fallah Seghrouchni, P. Taillibert, and C. Dinont, "A multi-agent system for resource privacy: Deployment of ambient applications in smart environments (extended abstract)," in Proceedings of the 2016 International Conference on Autonomous Agents, ser. AAMAS '16. International Foundation for Autonomous Agents and Multiagent Systems, 2016, pp. 1–2, ISBN: 9781450342391.

[8] G. Geetha and C. Jayakumar, "Implementation of trust and reputation management for free-roaming mobile agent security," IEEE Systems Journal, vol. 9, no. 2, June 2015, pp. 556–566, ISSN: 1932-8184.

[9] Y. Dong, N. Gupta, and N. Chopra, "Content modification attacks on consensus seeking multi-agent system with double-integrator dynamics," Chaos: An Interdisciplinary Journal of Nonlinear Science, vol. 26, no. 11, 2016, p. 116305. [Online]. Available: http://dx.doi.org/10.1063/1.4965034

[10] R. Gengarajoo, P. S.G., and C. K. Loo, Evaluating Trust in Multi-Agents System Through Temporal Difference Leaning. Springer International Publishing, 2016, pp. 513–524, ISBN: 9783319435060.

[11] T. I. Lab, "Java agent development framework," November 2016, URL: http://jade.tilab.com/ [accessed: 2017-03-10].

[12] R. Gitter, V. Lotz, and U. Pinsdorf, Security and legal force for mobile agents. Deutscher Universitäts-Verlag, 2007, ISBN: 9783824421732.

[13] O. Paracha, A Security Framework for Mobile Agent Systems, 2006, ISBN: 9781599427249.

[14] "Jade security guide," 2016, URL: http://www.jade.tilab.com/doc/tutorials/JADE_Security.pdf [accessed: 2017-03-10].

[15] A. P. Zonowski, "Jade-pki 1.0 manuel," November 2016, URL: http://jade.tilab.com/doc/tutorials/PKI_Guide.pdf [accessed: 2017-03-10].

[16] G. Vitaglione, "Mutual-authenticated ssl imtp connections," Dezember 2015, URL: http://jade.tilab.com/doc/tutorials/SSL-IMTP/SSL-IMTP.doc [accessed: 2017-03-10].

[17] C. Mitchell, Security for Mobility. Institution of Engineering and Technology, 2004, ISBN: 9780863413377.

[18] T. Bayer and C. Reich, "Proof of concept implementation of trusted agents," November 2016, URL: http://en.hs-furtwangen.de/fileadmin/userupload/IfCCITS/Dokumente/Publications/Theses/JADETrustedAgents.rar [accessed: 2017-03-10].

Semantic Models and Rule-based Reasoning for Fault Detection and Diagnostics: Applications in Heating, Ventilating and Air Conditioning Systems

Parastoo Delgoshaei and Mark A. Austin
Department of Civil and Environmental Engineering,
University of Maryland, College Park, MD 20742, USA
E-mail: parastoo@umd.edu; austin@isr.umd.edu

Daniel Veronica
National Institute of Standards and Technology (NIST),
Gaithersburg, MD 20899, USA
E-mail: daniel.veronica@nist.gov

Abstract—**This paper discusses an extensible model-based semantic framework for fault detection and diagnostics (FDD) in systems simulation and control. Generally speaking, state-of-the-art fault detection methods are equipment and domain specific. As a result, the applicability of these methods in different domains is very limited. Our proposed approach focuses on developing formal models (ontologies) across categories of domain-specific and domain-independent (time and space) phenomena. It then leverages inference-based reasoning over the ontologies for FDD purposes. Together, these techniques provide a semantic framework for the definition and evaluation of multidisplinary concepts relating to a system. FDD rules associated to those concepts are implemented as inference-based rules and are evaluated by a reasoner. We exercise the proposed method by looking at a FDD problem for heating, ventilating and air-conditioning (HVAC) systems simulation.**

Keywords-Fault Detection and Diagnostics; Ontology; Semantic; Rule-based; Heating Ventilating and Air-conditioning (HVAC) systems.

I. Introduction

A. Problem Statement

Automated fault detection and diagnostic (FDD) techniques provide mechanisms for condition-based maintenance of engineered systems (e.g., buildings, health monitoring, power plants and aviation systems). FDD is an automated process of detecting unwanted conditions ("faults") in these systems by recognizing deviations in real-time or recorded data values from expected values, and then diagnosing the causes leading to the faults. Proper implementation of FDD can enable proactive identification and remediation of faults before they become significantly deleterious to the safety, security, or efficiency of the operating system.

During the last decade, considerable research has focused on the development of FDD methods for HVAC&R systems. This work has been driven, in part, by the historically less-than-optimal operation of many state-of-the-art HVAC systems. Today, degraded or poorly-maintained equipment accounts for 15 to 30 % of energy consumption in commercial buildings [1]. Approximately 50 to 67 % of air conditioners (residential and commercial) are either improperly charged or have airflow issues [2] and [3]. Faulty heating, ventilating, air conditioning, and refrigeration (HVAC&R) systems contribute to 1.5 to 2.5 % of total commercial building consumption [4]. Much of this energy usage could be prevented by utilizing automated condition-based maintenance. Yet, in spite of recent advances in building automation and control, automatic methods for FDD of building systems remain at a relatively immature stage of development. Present-day fault diagnostic approaches are domain dependent and semantic-free.

B. Objectives and Scope

In a step toward overcoming these limitations, this paper proposes a semantic framework, composed of ontologies and rules sets, for fault detection and diagnostic analysis of HVAC systems. Our work employs the Web Ontology Language (OWL) [5] and Jena API [6] for the development of semantic models for FDD applications. A semantic model of FDD defines it in terms of inference-based rules expressing conditions within formal, domain-specific ontologies (e.g., mechanical equipment, building, and weather). The remainder of this paper proceeds as follows: Section II contains a brief introduction to the uses of the Semantic Web and its enabling technologies. Section III explains different methods of FDD in building system applications. Section IV describes the proposed methodology and software infrastructure, and a simple example for fault detection in a leaking hot water valve. Sections V and VI provide a discussion of the next steps and conclusions of the work to date.

II. The Semantic Web

A. Semantic Web Technology

The World Wide Web is almost thirty years old. Its initial mission was to provide a technical infrastructure for the representation of a "Web of documents and data" and presentation of data/content to humans [7]. In this infrastructure, machines are used primarily to retrieve and render information; humans are expected to interpret and understand the meaning of the content. A second, and much more ambitious, vision for the Web is support for semantic data structures, thereby allowing machines to access and share information, creating paths of machine-to-machine communications carrying semantic meanings instead of mere digital values. Realization of this goal requires mechanisms (i.e., markup languages) for the representation, coordination, and sharing of the formal semantics of data, as well as an ability to reason and draw conclusions (i.e., inference) from semantic data obtained by following hyperlinks to definitions of problem domains (i.e., ontology models).

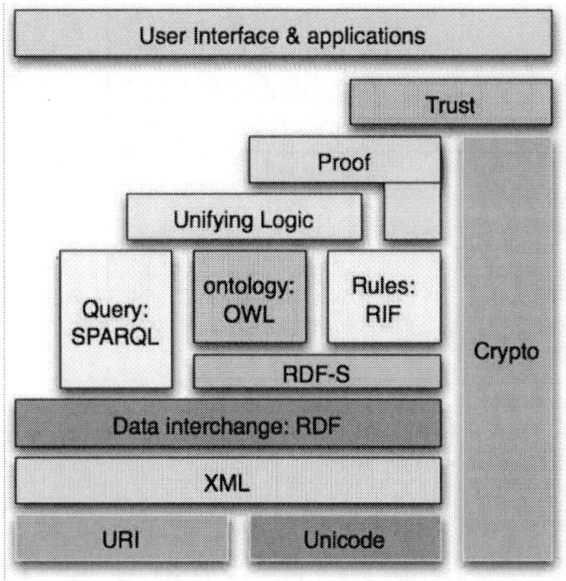

Figure 1. Technologies Used in Semantic Web Layers [8].

Figure 1 illustrates the layers of technologies supporting implementation of the Semantic Web [8]. Each higher layer extends, and provides compatibility with, layers of technology below it. The lower layers provide capability for addressing resources on the Web, linking documents, and integrating diverse forms of information. As a case in point, extended markup language (XML) enables the construction and management of documents composed of structured portable data. The resource description framework (RDF) allows for the modeling of graphs of resources on the Web. An RDF Schema (RDF-S) provides the basic vocabulary for RDF statements, and the machinery to create hierarchies of classes and properties. The Web Ontology Language (OWL) extends RDF-S by adding: (1) Advanced constructs to describe the semantics of RDF statements, (2) Vocabulary support for relationships between classes (e.g., class A is disjoint with class B), and (3) Restrictions on properties (e.g., cardinality). At higher levels of this stack, the ontology-based approach heavily relies on expressive features of the logic formalisms. For example, descriptive logic (DL) is the logical formalism for ontologies defined in OWL. Inference-based rules are rules that infer a new statement from existing statements. Inference-based rules rely on expressive features of the language they are defined in. Together, these features and language capabilities provide the foundations for reasoning - that is, deriving implicit conclusions not explicitly expressed in the ontology - using DL. In the Semantic Web, an inference engine gathers information from ontologies to infer the context that exists. Typically, the ontologies are defined in OWL or RDF-S.

B. Semantic Models

Semantic models consist of ontologies, graphs of individuals (specific instances), and rules derived from engineering models. An ontology represents the concepts of the domain (i.e., mechanical systems, building, weather, or occupant) as object classes, and the relationships between those classes as "Object Properties" (the connection between two objects of two classes). Moreover, the classes may have attributes that are stored as a simple data type "Datatype Properties". RDF-S and OWL are examples of an ontology DL. They provide ways to define the semantic relationships between concepts in an application domain, as well as the various contexts possible in that domain. The goal is a consistent system of ontological classes, properties, and interrelationships expressing the application domain in a language translatable into machine readable code. Such a language provides a means for the machine to effectively understand and reason about the contextual information. A context may refer to people, building, time, weather and so on. The proposition underlying our work is that Semantic Web technologies could be used for FDD applications in building systems.

III. FDD for Building Systems

Recent advances in building automation technologies provide a means for sensing and collecting the data needed for software applications to automatically detect and diagnose faults in buildings. During the past few decades a variety of FDD techniques have been developed in different domains, including model-based, rule-based, knowledge-based, and simulation-based approaches. Katipamula and Brambley summarizes FDD research for HVAC systems [1]. Their work also describes different fundamental FDD methods under the two main categories of model-based, and empirical (history-based) approaches. The major difference is in the nature of the knowledge used to formulate the diagnostics. Model-based diagnostics evaluate residuals between actual system measurements and *a priori* models (e.g., first principle models). Data-driven empirical strategies, on the other hand, do not require *a priori* models. The models used in model-based methods can be quantitative or qualitative. Quantitative models represent the requisite *a priori* knowledge of the system in terms of mathematical equations, typically as explicit descriptions of the physics underlying system components. Qualitative models, conversely, combine concepts such as descriptive "states" and "rules" into statements that are axiological instead of mathematical, expressing operational correctness or desirability through an axiology, a value system, appropriate to each physical application. As a result, the building system operation can be continuously classified as being either faulty or not faulty. Rule-based strategies are one example of qualitative model-based FDD methods. Rules can be based on first principles or they can be inferred from historical experiments, but in either case they represent expert qualitative knowledge that no purely quantitative representation could model. The first diagnostic expert systems for technical fault diagnosis were developed at MIT by Scherer and White [9]. Since then diagnostic systems have evolved from rule- to model-based approaches.

IV. Methods

Our methodology entails an ontology-based, inference-based extensible framework to store and reuse data across different applications and domains. This semantic approach has been adapted in the area of healthcare [11], biology [12], [13], and transportation [14]. This section describes how this

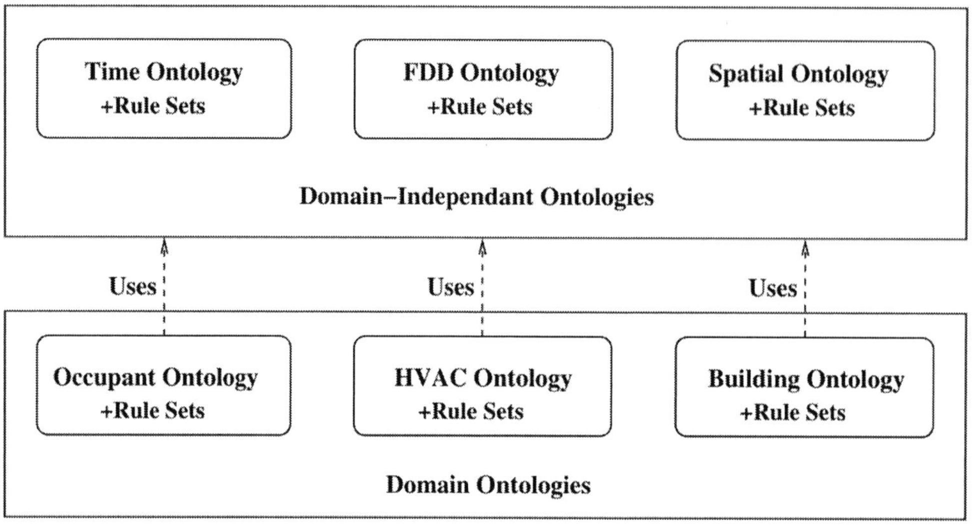

Figure 2. Domain specific and domain independent ontology structure .

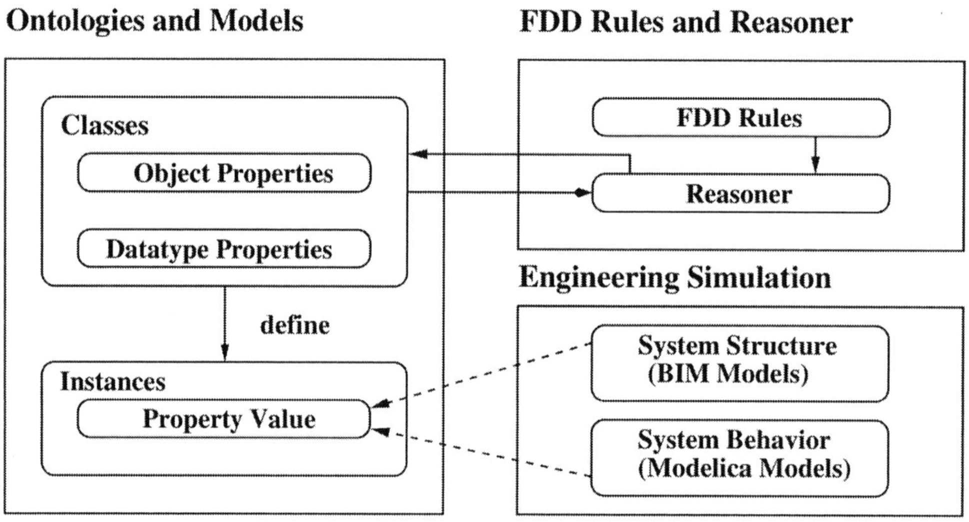

Figure 3. Architecture for coupled integrated semantic physical models in building simulations (Adapted from Delgoshaei, Austin and Pertzborn [10].

framework was utilized to formally model the concepts of the FDD domain.

A. Semantic Information Model

Figure 2 represents a semantic framework tailored for FDD and decision making within, and control of, engineered systems. Domain independent ontologies such as time, space, and FDD are represented in the upper half of the figure, and can be utilized in various engineering applications. For example, HVAC system ontologies along with their rule sets provide mechanisms to reason in time (e.g., if a measurement had occurred in a specific interval), deduce spatial information (e.g., determine if a room is in a specific zone or if a sensor is inside a room), and detect and diagnose faults (e.g., determine if a system fault is the result of leaking or stuck valve).

Figure 3 depicts the connection between the formal representation of a system and engineering models. On the building information modeling (BIM) side of the problem, a structural model of a building can be expressed in an ontology. As a case, Beetz and co-workers [15] have developed a converter to transform any format using EXPRESS schema, e.g., Industry Foundation Classes (IFC) into a Resource Description Framework (RDF) format. IFC is the standard used for BIM [16]. Moreover, to account for the behavior of the system, domain dependent ontologies (i.e., HVAC equipment) are based on models of the physical system and described in languages such as Modelica [17]. In this framework, the properties in the ontology represent the variables of the Modelica models that are updated at each time step. Ultimately, the real building sensors will provide the data to the ontologies.

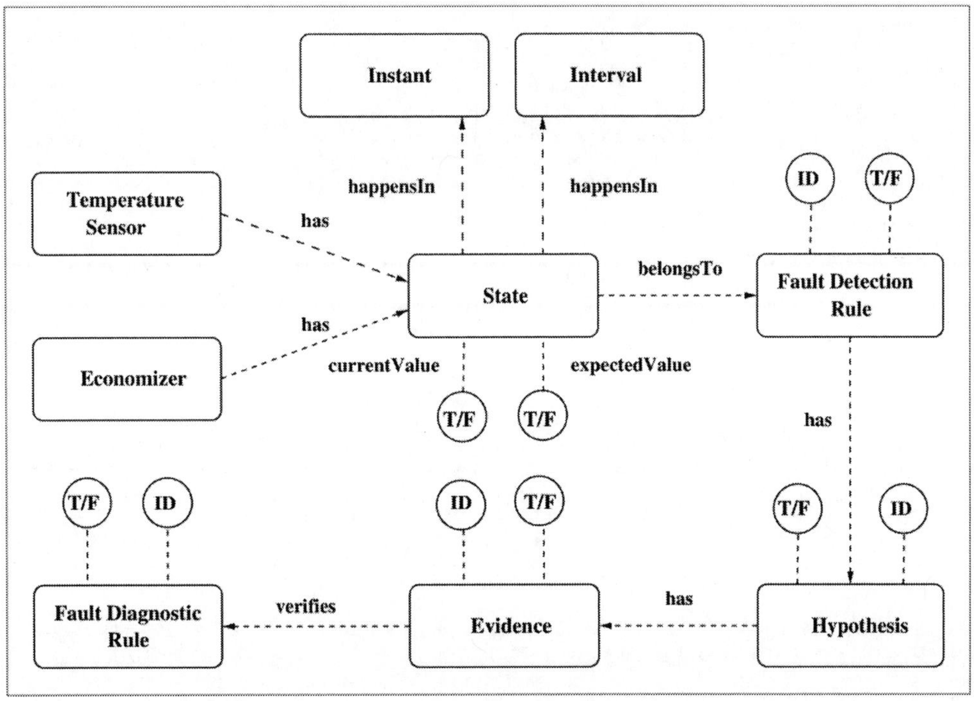

Figure 4. Domain specific and domain independent ontology structure.

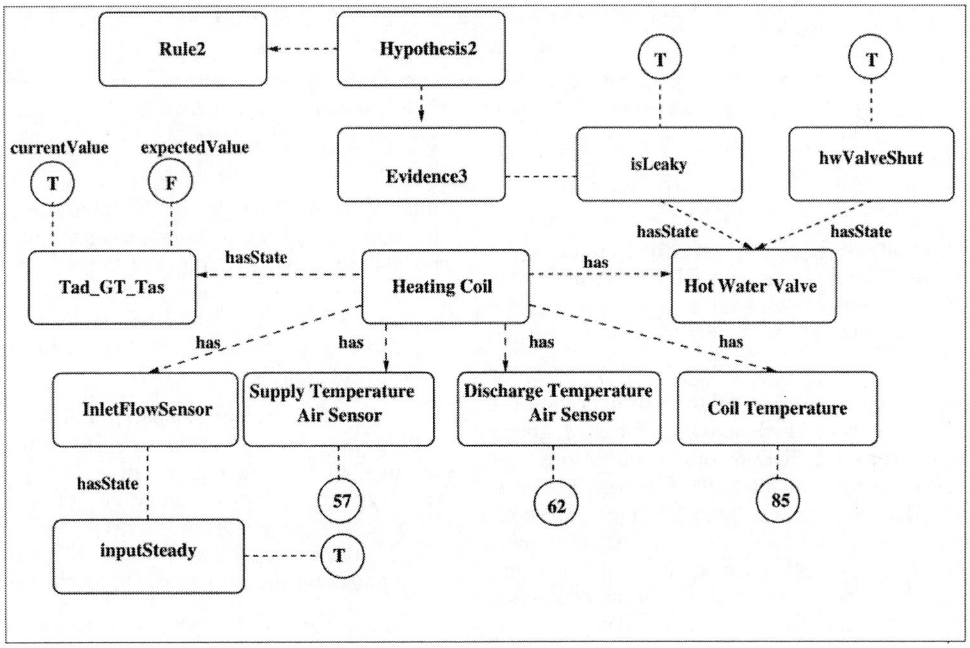

Figure 5. Subset of HVAC ontology at a specific instance of time.

TABLE I. Instances of states, hypotheses, and evidence for heating coil fault detections.

```
State          inputSteady
                hwValveShut
                Tad_GT_Tas
                isLeaky

Hypothesis1    HWVDFail         --> Hot Water Valve Drive Failure.
Hypothesis2    HWLeakValve      --> Hot Water Valve Leaking.
Hypothesis2    TadSensorFail    --> Temperature, air, discharge (Tad) sensor bad.
Hypothesis3    TasSensorFail    --> Temperature, air, supply (Tas) sensor bad.

Evidence3      Coil metal temperature is above Tas
```

Pseudo Jena Rules

```
Rule 1: Assignment rule:

[Rule1: (?c rdf:type eq:Coil) (?c eq:Tad ?v1) (?c eq:Tas ?v2) greaterThan(?v2, ?v1) ->
        (?c eq:Tad_GT_Tas "true" )  ]

Rule 2: Expectation rule:

[Rule2: (?c1 rdf:type eq:sensor) (?c1 FDD:inputSteady "true") (?c2 rdf:type eq:valve)
        (?c2  "hwValveCommandedShut''  "true'') -> (?c3 rdf:type eq:tempSensor) (?s3 rdf:type FDD:State)
        equal(?s3  "Tad_GT_Tas'') (?s3 FDD:expectedValue "false" ) (?s3 FDD:belongsTo "Rule2'' ]

Rule 3: Detection rule:

[Rule3: (?c rdf:type component) (?c FDD:hasState ?s)(?s  FDD:belongsTo ?r) (?s   FDD:expectedState ?es)
        (?s FDD:currentState ?cs) notEqual(?es ?cs) -> (?r FDD:isViolated "true") ]

Rules 4 and 5: Diagnostic rules:

[Rule4: (?r rdf:type rule2) (?r rdf:type evidence3) -> (?h rdf:type hypothesis2)

[Rule5: (?hwv rdf:type valve) (?hwv FDD:shut  "true") (?c rdf:type Coil)
        (?c eq:hasValve ?hwv) (?c FDD:metalTemp ?t1) (?c FDD:Tas ?t2) greaterThan(?t2  ?t1) ->
        (?hwv eq:isLeaky "true") (evidence3  "true" ) ]
```

Figure 6. Fault detection diagnostic rules for operation of a heating coil.

B. Support for Reasoning and Inference

Reasoning and inference are the powerful features of this semantic framework. The inferences are achieved through rules and a reasoner called upon by an engine, which executes the rules and updates the ontology with new inferences that may result.

Diagnostic procedures are required to have hypotheses of the underlying cause-effect relationships, and for our purposes these are represented by the FDD ontology and its rule sets. Figure 4 is a close-up view of the FDD ontology. The main concepts of the FDD ontology are "State", "Rule", "Hypothesis", and "Evidence." These concepts are related to each other as object properties. Notice that the concept "Detection Rule" is related to the concept "Hypothesis" through the object property "has"; the concepts "Evidence" and "Hypothesis" are linked through the object property "verifies." Also notice that "State" has two boolean datatype properties, "CurrentValue" and "ExpectedValue." A few examples of different individuals in the class "State" include: temperature being within a specific band (T/F) and economizer mode in effect (T/F).

In the FDD ontology there are different categories for the rules. The first category of the inference rules is responsible for setting the current states associated with the system components (assignment). Some of these states will be computed based on function evaluations. As a case in point, a built-in function is called to perform the analysis and determination of the value for the boolean state "The temperature is going back to where it was."

The second category, expectation rules, are responsible for setting expected values for the states if certain conditions are met. In other words, if certain states (antecedent) of the ontology are true, then some other states of the ontology (consequent) are expected to also be true. As a case in point, if the outside temperature is within a specific range (T), then an economizer mode is expected to be in effect (T).

Lastly, the third category of rules is responsible for detecting and diagnosing the faults. The detection process is achieved by comparing the results of current values of a state with the expected values of a state. The diagnostics process is achieved by identifying what evidence holds true and as a result, which hypothesis accounts for the fault.

C. Fault Detection for a Leaking Hot Water Valve

Table I summarizes the list of examples for the class of the FDD concepts shown in Figure 5, a subset of the HVAC ontology with the values of individuals stored in the ontological graph at a specific time. Specifically, it represents a case where a fault has occurred in the system due to a leaking hot water valve.

The execution of rules in the heating coil operation involves four steps. Step 1, the assignment rule: If the discharge air temperature is greater than the supply temperature, then Tad_GT_Tas is set to true, e.g., Rule 1. Step 2, the expectation rule: If the unit has been operating steadily for a specified interval, and the hot water valve is shut, the mean value of discharge air temperature is expected to be less than or equal to the mean of supply air temperature (e.g., Rule 2). Step 3, the detection rule: When the current value of a specific state is not equal to its expected value, then the associated rule is violated (e.g., Rule 3). The final step is a diagnostic rule: If the coil metal temperature is above Tas twenty minutes after the hot water valve is manually driven shut, then the shut valve is still leaking. This presents a significant use of heating energy.

While it is perfectly reasonable to expect that the state variable values will change as a function of time, the expected values in a specific rule will stay constant, and act as the point of reference for detecting faults. As an example, a rule is defined to detect whether a specific piece of HVAC equipment is responding properly to conditions in the rooms it serves. If the data ordinarily sampled do not indicate the equipment is making the proper response (i.e., it "fails" the rule), the engine calls on the reasoner and expert knowledge to use deeper, more extraordinarily obtained data (evidence) to infer a cause (hypothesis) for the improper response.

Figure 6 shows the pseudo Jena rules described over the FDD, Equipment (eq) ontologies. The current value for the state Tad_GT_Tas is determined based on Rule1. Rule 2, sets the expected value for Tad_GT_Tas when the valve is shut off and will set the associated detection rule (rule2). Rule 3 detects the fault. Rule 4, asserts if Evidence3 holds, Hypothesis 3 that the valve is leaking holds true. Rule 5, describes how the values for flow and temperature sensors will determined if Evidence3 holds true.

V. Discussion

The proposed approach is a first step in the development of a model-based semantic framework for FDD. State-of-the-art techniques for FDD in buildings lack real-time rule-checking. Consequently, there is always a lag between the fault detection and potential diagnostics and decision-making. Our position is that developing ontologies for different categories of domain-specific and domain-independent faults facilitates FDD in HVAC system simulation and controls.

VI. Conclusion and Future Work

This paper demonstrates a model-based semantic framework for automated fault detection and diagnostics (FDD) for application to building controls, specifically heating, ventilating and air-conditioning (HVAC). Our preliminary results are promising and indicate that future building control strategies could utilize formal models (ontologies and rules) for the detection of a variety of types of fault. To make building simulations and fault diagnostic procedures more realistic, however, our capability needs to be extended toward real-time simulation and decision making. Our plans are to deploy the proposed method for an actual case study problem, and use the buildings library Modelica models.

VII. Acknowledgment

The first author was supported by a fellowship award from the NIST Graduate Student Measurement Science and Engineering (GMSE) Program.

References

[1] S. Katipamula and M. R. Brambley, "Review Article: Methods for Fault Detection, Diagnostics, and Prognostics for Building SystemsA Review, Part I," HVAC&R Research, vol. 11, no. 1, 2005, pp. 3–25.

[2] J. A. Siegel and C. P. Wray, "An Evaluation of Superheat-based Refrigerant Charge Diagnostics for Residential Cooling Systems/Discussions," ASHRAE Transactions 108(1), 2002, p. 965.

[3] W. Kim and J. E. Braun, "Impacts of refrigerant charge on air conditioner and heat pump performance," in Impacts of Refrigerant Charge on Air Conditioner and Heat Pump Performance, July 10–15 2010, pp. 2433–2441.

[4] M. Wiggins and J. Brodrick, "Emerging Technologies: HVAC Fault Detection," ASHRAE Journal, April 2012, pp. 78–80.

[5] OWL:, "Web Ontology Language Overview, W3C Recommendation from February, 2004. For details, see http://www.w3.org/TR/owl-features/ (Accessed, April 2017)."

[6] Apache Jena, "An Open Source Java Framework for building Semantic Web and Linked Data Applications, Accessible at https://jena.apache.org (Accessed on 12/12/16)," 2016.

[7] T. Berners-Lee, J. Hendler and O. Lassila, "The Semantic Web," Scientific American, May 2001, pp. 28–37.

[8] L. Feigenbaum, 2006, Semantic Web Technologies in the Enterprise.

[9] W. T. Scherer and C. C. White, A Survey of Expert Systems for Equipment Maintenance and Diagnostics. Boston, MA: Springer US, 1989, pp. 285–300.

[10] P. Delgoshaei, M. A. Austin and A. Pertzborn, "A Semantic Framework for Modeling and Simulation of Cyber-Physical Systems," International Journal On Advances in Systems and Measurements, vol. 7, no. 3-4, December 2014, pp. 223–238.

[11] T. Q. Dung and W. Kameyama, Ontology-based Information Extraction and Information Retrieval in Health Care Domain, ser. Lecture Notes in Computer Science (including subseries Lecture Notes in Artificial Intelligence and Lecture Notes in Bioinformatics), 2007, vol. 4654 LNCS, pp. 323–333.

[12] C. Taswell, "DOORS to the Semantic Web and Grid with a PORTAL for Biomedical Computing," IEEE Trans Inf Technol Biomed, vol. 12, no. 2, 2008, pp. 191–204.

[13] P. Lord, S. Bechhofer, M. D. Wilkinson, G. Schiltz, D. Gessler, D. Hull, C. Goble, and L. Stein, Applying Semantic Web Services to Bioinformatics: Experiences Gained, Lessons Learnt. Berlin, Heidelberg: Springer Berlin Heidelberg, 2004, pp. 350–364.

[14] D. Corsar, D. Milan, P. Edwards, and J. D. Nelson, The Transport Disruption Ontology. Lecture Notes in Computer Science, vol 9367, Springer, 2015, pp. 329–336.

[15] J. Beetz, J. van Leeuwen and B. de Vries, "IfcOWL: A Case of Transforming EXPRESS Schemas into Ontologies," Artificial Intelligence for Engineering Design, Analysis and Manufacturing, vol. 23, no. 1, 2009, pp. 89–101.

[16] C. M. Eastman, P. Techolz, R. Sacks and K. Liston, BIM Handbook: A Guide to Building Information Modeling. Hoboken, NJ: John-Wiley and Sons, 2008.

[17] P. Fritzson, Principles of Object-Oriented Modeling and Simulation with Modelica 2.1. Wiley-IEEE Press, 2003.

Scoring Methods to Enable Bespoke Portfolio Management

Daniel Pashley
Industrial Doctorate Centre in Systems
University of Bristol
Bristol, UK
Email: dp13092@bristol.ac.uk

Theodore Tryfonas, Andrew Crossley
Department of Civil Engineering
University of Bristol
Bristol, UK
Email: {theo.tryfonas, andrew.crossley}@bristol.ac.uk

Chris Setchell
Imetrum Limited
Bristol, UK
Email: chris.setchell@imetrum.com

Abstract— **To achieve competitive advantage, many companies need to engage and invest in Research and Development. For this investment to be effective, resources need to be allocated appropriately across all projects. However, when the portfolio of the company is diverse or large, this assignment can be challenging. Portfolio Management has been created as a method for companies to effectively manage new, existing and potential projects. Yet, these methods can introduce bias and subjectivity without being flexible to the pieces of information, or attributes that are important to the company. This work adds to the field by proposing three scoring methods that convert any attribute into a numerical representation that can then be used for comparison. For managers, it means that they can select any attributes of importance to them to allow their portfolio to be prioritised and have the resource allocated appropriately to the projects that offer the greatest promise.**

Keywords- Portfolio Management; New Product Development; Scoring; Prioritisation

I. Introduction

Businesses often form their strategy around the development of new products [1]. This can take several forms including radical [2], incremental [1] and disruptive [3]. These different strategies lead to a number of products making up the company's portfolio [4]. The difficulty for companies comes from selecting which of the next generation of potential developments should become reality and join the existing portfolio [5].

Currently there are a number of tools available to companies to aid this selection process including those presented in [6]–[8]. However, these methods introduce the potential for subjectivity, bias and an undue focus on particular attributes such as those defined by monetary values, when others may be of greater use to the company. This research and paper focus on proposing three new methods to evaluate potential development projects that can be combined to form key elements of a Portfolio Management process.

During the process of identifying new development projects, capturing and understanding information is critical. Therefore, identifying the information which is most critical makes up a core part of this process. Utilising a process of identification from a company's perspective as to which are the most critical pieces of information can allow for directed capture and review. This forms a simple process, especially from the small and medium sized enterprise perspective of limited resource [1], which can result in clear understanding via prioritisation of the options available to them.

From this point, the paper takes the following structure. In Section 2, the background literature on the topic will be investigated including Portfolio Management and the tools that make up these methods. Next, in Section 3, the proposed three methods will be presented along with how they can be combined into a single process. Examples will make up part of these descriptions. Finally, in Section 4, the presented methods and process will be discussed before concluding.

II. Background Literature

Many firms rely on Research and Development (R&D) to achieve a competitive position within their market [2]. The challenge associated with this is assessing these opportunities [3] so the available resources can be distributed appropriately to ensure the selected projects can begin and continue. With limited resources, which is always a concern, effectively managing the development pipeline is critical [4]. This helps to maximise returns by only allowing appropriate projects to begin. Within business, this distribution of resource is a managerial decision [5]. As such, the decision requires the necessary attention being placed on planning and understanding projects.

It is not uncommon for several options to present themselves at the same time or to be implemented together [5] alongside existing projects. However, the difficulty with initiating new projects originates from not knowing which will be a success [3]. So the question becomes " how to do the correct projects?" [2]. One approach is to use a conceptual funnel [6] which narrows down all potential projects into those with a higher chance of success. Within this conceptual funnel, activities such as investigation, evaluation and prioritising of potential projects are conducted [4]. By prioritising potential projects as part of the conceptual funnel allows for an appropriate distribution of resources [2] to those projects that warrant them more. Approaches that are used to do this are either quantitative or qualitative using methods that range from rigorous tests to social-science methods [3].

A prominent approach to aid in the management of active and potential projects is Portfolio Management [7]. This has been developed to coordinate multiple projects towards the same strategic goals [8] and is commonly used to manage the composition of a company's product portfolio, including potential new product development [7]. This is commonly used in a planning capacity by managers or key players in an organisation [7] and ties into the management of the development pipeline [4]. As a part of this process, a primary filter can be used to draw attention to particular potential projects [9] based on attributes such as their market potential. This can aid in removing those potential projects that would not deliver on their promise or are only pitched due to internal political reasons [2]. Portfolio Management is a way in which information about potential projects is gathered and prioritised [7] such that only the most worthy are chosen to become part of the company's product portfolio.

There are several methods and frameworks discussed in literature for Portfolio Management. A method presented in [9] utilises scoring a potential project with respect to a number of criteria. However, when these same criteria are given to multiple people for review there is the strong possibility for different results to be returned due to their individual experience, making this highly subjective. The risk-reward matrix is also presented in [9] with the most desirable case being to have a project that is both low risk and high reward. Other methods include the organisation wide selection process in [10], the data envelopment analysis and balance scorecard method in [11]. Additional methods are also presented in [2], [3], [12].

When using the presented methods, decision attributes that are commonly used are cost-benefit and cash-flow [12]. These are converted into a single determinant, such as Net Present Value (NPV) or Internal Rate of Return (IRR) [2] so that they can be readily compared. However, there are several attributes that are unable to be converted into a financial measure. These include risk, route to market and engagement opportunities; all critical aspects to understand in relation to a potential technology development. Therefore, by using only financial measures, only half the picture is seen [13]; whereas by using other attributes a more holistic view is attained. Conventionally it is not possible to represent certain attributes using a single financial measure as they are not an amount of money as they are more conceptual; furthermore they can be highly subjective.

III. Proposed Scoring Method and Portfolio Management Process

Scoring has been a project selection technique since its origin in the 1950's [9]. Scoring methods help to estimate how attractive a project is and which path to take [14]. In addition, these methods present sufficient rigor while not being overly complex to discourage use [9]. Furthermore, they can also accommodate non-quantitative or "fuzzy" and non-detailed data whilst also being customised for the organisation they are deployed in [9].

To construct the proposed scoring methods, three key properties were identified to differentiate between types of attribute and therefore which method can be used to apply a score. These properties are Independent, Comparable and Bounded. Independent refers to the ability of an attribute to be scored in isolation, with the score it receives being in no way related to those before or relying on those from another attribute. Comparable means that the only way to effectively score an attribute is through comparing it to several other instances. Bounded relates to the possible inputs that can be associated to that attribute, which can be of any value but will always be between two points, i.e., maximum and minimum.

TABLE I. POSSIBLE PROPERTY COMBINATIONS

Combination	Independent (I)	Comparable (C)	Bounded (B)
1	Y	Y	Y
2	Y	Y	N
3	Y	N	Y
4	Y	N	N
5	N	Y	Y
6	N	N	Y
7	N	Y	N
8	N	N	N

Not all the combinations described in TABLE I are possible to be applied together. Combination 1 cannot occur due to attributes not being able to be both Independent and Comparable together as these properties do not align. Combination 2 and 4 are not possible as an Independent parameter, that is also non Bounded, would effectively change each time it is used and would therefore require older versions to be changed, making it none Independent. Finally, combination 6 and 8 are not possible as an attribute can be neither Independent nor Comparable, as they have to be mutually exclusive. This leaves combinations 3, 5 and 7. Each of these combinations derives to make a viable method of applying a score to attributes.

TABLE II. SCORING METHODS BASED ON PROPERTY COMBINATIONS

Method	Combination	I	C	B
Absolute	3	Y	N	Y
Balance	7	N	Y	N
Comparative	5	N	Y	Y

Each of the methods shown in TABLE II will now be presented along with an example demonstrating their use.

A. *Absolute*

This method is the most straight forward of all those proposed and is to be used with attributes that can be used in isolation, i.e., have no direct bearing on others. Furthermore, they can use a simple grading method with a series of criteria and associated scores where the user selects the one which matches the closest. Once the score is applied, it stands irrespective of other attributes, whether they are new or existing.

Associated with each of these criteria is a Normalised Score on the scale desired, 1 – 5 for example. Therefore, by selecting the criteria that best fits with the current attribute, a score is applied. Each criterion then becomes the Normalised Score that can be applied to the attributes.

The steps for this method can be summarised as follows:

1. Define question
2. Define range of responses
3. Select answer from responses
4. Value associated with response assigned as the score

1) Absolute example

An example for a use of the Absolute method is the number of geographical regions that a new product could enter. This could be a range between 1 – 6 for how many regions out of Europe, North America, South America, Africa, Asia and Australasia a new product could be marketed in. Such an example is similarly demonstrated in [14] who discuss the effective commercialisation required when selecting appropriate markets for a new product. Therefore by implementing this metric, they would be more certain of a technology to succeed in multiple markets, demonstrating its worth over others. An example of this could be as follows:

"How many regions out of Europe, North America, South America, Africa, Asia and Australasia can the new technology enter?"

1	2	3	4	5	6

Figure 1. Example regions to enter

In this case, the number of regions which the innovation could enter, selected via Figure 1, can be directly related to the score that is applied; with the more regions that can be entered reflecting the higher the absolute score.

B. *Balance*

The Balance method makes use of a Normalised Scale; this is represented by a number scale which is defined by the user and is the range of values that the resulting scores can take. An example would range between 1 and 5 with increments of 1; meaning the scale has five possible values that scored attributes can take. These points on the Normalised Scale then become the Normalised Scores assigned to the attributes.

This method is one which is utilised when the attributes are unable to be scored independently and have to be compared to all values entered previously; an example of this could be the expected return from a product whereby a new market entry has the potential to be far more lucrative than current markets. Therefore to utilise this method, a value for the new attribute is entered by the user, and a comparison is then made between it and existing values. As the new values are unbounded, i.e., can be of any size, attention needs to be placed on their magnitude such that the values that are significantly larger or smaller are normalised.

The balance is defined between two values with set increments between the Normalised Score marks. In all cases with this method, once there are sufficient values (more than one), the upper and lower bound values (5 and 50 for example) are placed in either extreme on the scale as demonstrated in Figure 2.

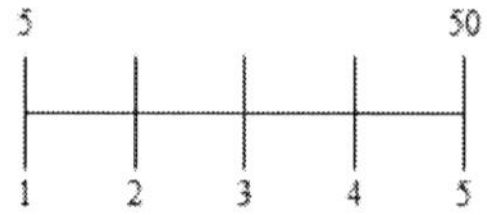

Figure 2. Balance method Normalised Scale

Following this, for any subsequent values entered a series of steps are to be followed to allow for the new value to be placed accordingly. With the upper and lower bounds defined, the difference between them is calculated and divided by the number of steps between them. This Step Change value is added onto the lower bound accumulatively for each step until the upper bound is reached, as shown in Figure 3. These new step values represent what each attribute has to exceed to achieve a certain Normalised Score.

$$Step\ Change = \frac{(50 - 5)}{4} = 11.5 \quad (1)$$

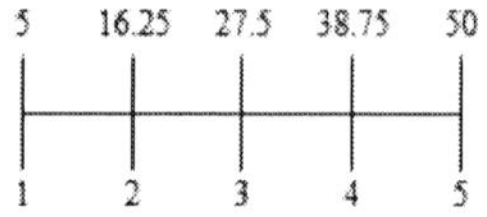

Figure 3. Distributed Step Change value onto Normalised Scale

With the upper and lower bounds set and the Step Change applied to each point on the Normalised Scale, any values entered between these points now fall onto this scale. For example, if a new value was added of 20, this would fit in between 2 and 3 on the Normalised Scale, rounding its Normalised Score down to 2.

The advantage of using this method for such values is that it can cater for any value to be added of any size. These values are then distributed such that the resulting Normalised Score reflects their magnitude. Additionally, if a new value is added of significantly different size, either larger or smaller, the distribution of values is adjusted to reflect this. An example would be where a new value is added, which is significantly smaller, all values are re-distributed up the scale and likewise if a value is entered of significantly larger size, they are re-distributed down the scale. A way to think of this method is by picturing a seesaw; when something with a much larger weight is added (larger value), it tilts in that direction (positive or negative) with respect to the difference in weight (size of value) to that already on it.

The process for this method is:

1. Define range
2. Define increments
3. Calculate result
4. Enter result
5. Assign values automatically if insufficient
6. Or Else, assign minimum and maximum values
7. Calculate Step Change
8. Calculate Normalised Scores
9. Store results

1) Balance example

An example for the Balance method is scoring costs as these values are unbounded and can take any size. For example, if common values are between £10 and £100, but a new value is added of £200, the magnitude of the difference needs to be reflected. In business it is common to conduct investigations into potential developments before conducting any further work into them, such as in the automotive example presented in [15]; whereby they analyse the costs of new automotive products before selecting a development path. This can be combined with that presented in [16], where estimating the cost of a new development before conducting any work, illustrates effective portfolio management.

For example, a user is generating scores based on estimates for market size for a potential technology they could make. Through a simple calculation, approximate values for this can be calculated and entered into the Balance scoring method. Assume that £1m, £2m, £3m, £4m and £5m have already been entered as shown in Figure 4.

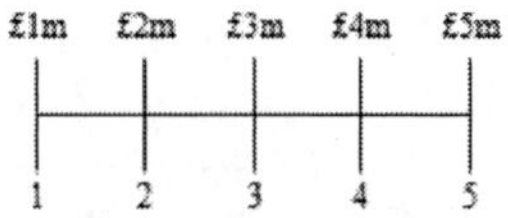

Figure 4. Example Balanced method scale

a. **Entered values are shown on the top, with Normalised Scores on the bottom**

However, if there is a new potential technology that can be made which has a potential market of £10m; this is significantly higher than those already entered. By adding a value of £10m to those already scored, the distribution and the required score to reach the next score boundary changes. This new distribution and assigned scores are shown in Figure 5.

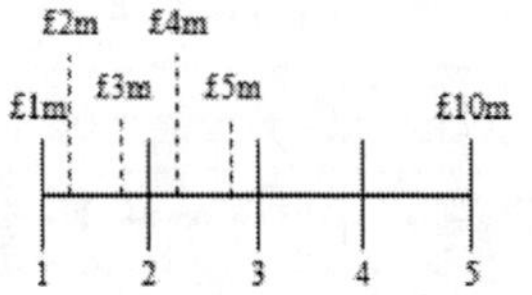

Figure 5. Expanded example of Balance method scale

Figure 5 demonstrates how the addition of a 6th, much larger value onto the scale results in existing values having to shift downwards to accommodate it.

As can be seen, through the addition of unbounded scoring values such as cost or value, there can be a relative shift in the resulting score based on its magnitude. This can be beneficial, as the relative difference is important to demonstrate an attributes worth over the others.

C. Comparative

The Comparative method also makes use of a Normalised Scale and is used when an attribute cannot be treated in isolation. Furthermore, it is designed to be used with those attributes that are more abstract or "fuzzy" and therefore difficult to score directly and instead are scored by comparing them to others. To allow an attribute of this type to be graded, a simple comparison is conducted between several attributes. Those to be used in the comparison are selected to represent a spread of scores such that it can be conducted against all levels of result, not just a single point. The spread of the comparable attributes is determined by the range of the final normalised range of scores to represent the extremes and several intervals in between. In total four existing attributes are selected to be used for the comparison so that when combined with the new attribute, there is a total of five. If there are insufficient existing attributes to facilitate this number for the comparison, select as many as are available and in the case of one attribute assign the middle Normalised Score. The selected attributes, along with that to be scored, are arranged so a pairwise comparison can be conducted so that all attributes are compared to each other. The underlying method that conducts the pairwise comparison is the Analytic Hierarchy

Process [17]–[19], which uses a four point scale around a midpoint towards each attribute being compared. This demonstrates a graded preference to neither or one of the attributes. Following the completion of the comparisons, a maximum score of 1 is given when all five attributes are selected, and a score for each attribute is calculated. These new scores then update those held for each attribute, as they have been compared to a new attribute and thus their former calculated score is no longer valid. A method for conducting this pairwise comparison is shown in Figure 6, which utilises Microsoft Excel to present the required information to the user.

Current score												Current score	Score
	T5	-9	-7	-5	-3	1	3	5	7	9	T1	5	1
	T5	-9	-7	-5	-3	1	3	5	7	9	T2	4	1
	T5	-9	-7	-5	-3	1	3	5	7	9	T3	2	1
	T5	-9	-7	-5	-3	1	3	5	7	9	T4	1	1
5	T1	-9	-7	-5	-3	1	3	5	7	9	T2	4	1
5	T1	-9	-7	-5	-3	1	3	5	7	9	T3	2	1
5	T1	-9	-7	-5	-3	1	3	5	7	9	T4	1	1
4	T2	-9	-7	-5	-3	1	3	5	7	9	T3	2	1
4	T2	-9	-7	-5	-3	1	3	5	7	9	T4	1	1
2	T3	-9	-7	-5	-3	1	3	5	7	9	T4	1	1

Figure 6. Example Comparison between attributes shown in Microsoft Excel

a. Technology abbreviated to T

Result	
Technology 1	0.2
Technology 2	0.2
Technology 3	0.2
Technology 4	0.2
Technology 5	0.2

Figure 7. Results from attribute comparison shown in Microsoft Excel

Now that the new Analytic Hierarchy Process scores have been calculated relative to the newly added attribute as per Figure 7, the ranking for all attributes and the final Normalised Scale will be changed. To do this a Normalised Scale is used that acts with bounded upper and lower values and an even distribution in between where the user defines the overall size of the scale and the increments between the steps i.e., 1-5 and with a spacing of 1. This method assigns values by initially (when there are insufficient values to occupy all spaces) entering them ranked around the centre of the scale until all spaces are occupied. Following this, the upper and lower bounds are positioned and the remaining values are evenly distributed between these positions, with the space they fall into always being rounded down to the lower bound to award the Normalised Score.

This method of applying scores via an even distribution of values between two extremes is done due to the way the values being entered are bounded between 0 and 1 from the Analytic Hierarchy Process.

The outline for this method is:

1. Define range
2. Define increments
3. Select other paths to compare to
4. Conduct comparison
5. Calculate Analytic Hierarchy Process score
6. Update results
7. Evenly distribute on Normalised Score
8. Update Normalised Scores

1) Comparative example

An example of an attribute that would require the Comparative method would be the risk in relation to developing a new technology. This type of attribute is something that is "fuzzy" and that is difficult to define explicitly in isolation and is therefore easier to compare to others. Such a comparison is presented by [20], [21] for exactly this purpose; risk is a difficult attribute to define, therefore it is best done through a comparison with others. By directly comparing multiple examples of the same attribute, a gauge of the risk can be created.

In this example, the risk associated with creating a new technology (T5) is to be compared with those already analysed, with the question for this comparison being "In each comparison, which technologies development presents the most risk?"

Current score												Current score	Score
	T5	-9	-7	-5	-3	1	3	5	7	9	T1	5	-9
	T5	-9	-7	-5	-3	1	3	5	7	9	T2	4	-5
	T5	-9	-7	-5	-3	1	3	5	7	9	T3	2	3
	T5	-9	-7	-5	-3	1	3	5	7	9	T4	1	1
5	T1	-9	-7	-5	-3	1	3	5	7	9	T2	4	-7
5	T1	-9	-7	-5	-3	1	3	5	7	9	T3	2	7
5	T1	-9	-7	-5	-3	1	3	5	7	9	T4	1	3
4	T2	-9	-7	-5	-3	1	3	5	7	9	T3	2	5
4	T2	-9	-7	-5	-3	1	3	5	7	9	T4	1	-3
2	T3	-9	-7	-5	-3	1	3	5	7	9	T4	1	-3

Figure 8. Example comparison of development risk shown in Microsoft Excel

a. Technology abbreviated to T

In Figure 8, it can be seen how the risk in the development of each technology has been compared. With the results from these comparisons, a calculation is done automatically to create the Analytic Hierarchy Process score for each technology being compared.

Result	
Technology 3	0.344428
Technology 5	0.22468
Technology 4	0.189694
Technology 2	0.124421
Technology 1	0.11677

Figure 9. Analytic Hierarchy Process score for Comparative method

With these newly calculated scores, shown in Figure 9, the database containing scores for all technologies is updated to reflect this change to these items. Following this, all values are distributed evenly on a defined Normalised Scale, between 1 and 5 for example, with respect to the largest and smallest values.

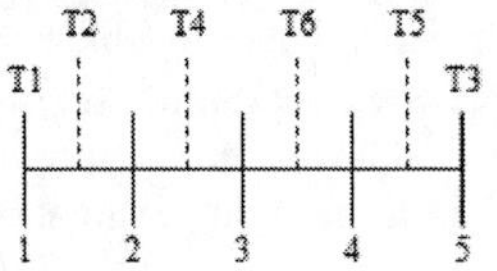

Figure 10. Comparative method scale

a. Technology abbreviated to T

The scale presented in Figure 10 demonstrates how the scores assigned to the technologies are ranked with the use of a Normalised Scale. In this example, an additional technologies score (T6) is also added as this was previously calculated and not selected to be part of the comparison. These scores are distributed with the upper and lower scores first and the remaining scores in order, evenly between these points.

This example shows how the Comparative method can be used to relate a score that can be used as a representation for a "fuzzy" concept such as the risk associated with a concept such as a new technologies development. Therefore, this effectively removed the difficulty in assigning a score to represent an attribute that reflects the addition of more values in the future.

D. *Proposed portfolio management process*

Based on the descriptions of the three scoring methods it can be seen how any attribute in relation to a potential development project can be scored to give a numerical value to represent it. Therefore, using these three methods, a process can be designed that can be used by any company to investigate, evaluate and prioritise potential development projects.

During the identification phase, the attributes that are of importance to the company need to be identified. These can typically include cost, value to the user, risk of development, commercial risk, competition and route to market. As the scoring methods all allow for complex attributes to be converted into a numerical form, they can applied to any attribute that is important to consider. By identifying key attributes the investigation process into the potential development can be enhanced and directed.

TABLE II can be used to align these identified attributes to the correct scoring method. Once the alignment to a scoring method has been completed, the questions, responses and Normalised Scales and Scores need to be recorded. Following this, the review is conducted based on the captured information as directed by the selected attributes.

The scores for each attribute, relating to each potential development project, are aggregated to create its total score. These scores can then be directly compared to those relating to other potential development projects, as they have been investigated and scored using the same attributes. One way to conduct this comparison is by ranking the potential development projects by these scores, giving then an R&D priority.

TABLE III. EXAMPLE AGGREGATE SCORES

Potential development project	Aggregate score
Technology 2	27
Technology 4	25
Technology 1	20
Technology 5	14
Technology 3	6

A threshold value can then be used to distribute resources to the potential development projects that display the required level of promise. By using the possible Normalised Scores for each of the attributes, as defined earlier in the process, a threshold value that has to be achieved before resources are allocated can also be defined. For example, if the maximum possible score for a potential development project is 30, the lowest threshold value to be achieved could be set as 20. This would serve as an indication for the managers tasked with Portfolio Management as to which potential development projects can deliver the required investment and resource utilisation confidence before funding them further.

TABLE IV. EXAMPLE AGGREGATE SCORES USING A THRESHOLD

Potential development project	Aggregate score
Technology 2	27
Technology 4	25
Technology 1	20
Technology 5	14
Technology 3	6

As can be seen in TABLE IV, by using a threshold approach gives a clear indication to the potential development projects that can deliver the most confidence of success. The threshold of 20 is shown by the thick horizontal line meaning potential development projects for Technologies 2, 4 and 1 should be allocated resources in that respective order. Technology 5 and 3 do not make the required threshold to be allocated resource.

This overall process of utilising the three scoring methods for Portfolio Management has been named the ABC Threshold approach. This is reflective of the three methods (Absolute, Balance and Comparative) used to investigate, evaluate and prioritise potential development projects with respect to the specific needs and situation of the company with the use of the threshold value.

The ABC threshold approach can be outlined as follows:

1. Identify attributes of importance
2. Align them to the correct scoring method
3. Conduct the review
4. Prioritise them based on the value

5. Apply threshold

The process described here is reflected in Figure 11 which demonstrates the flow between the required stages.

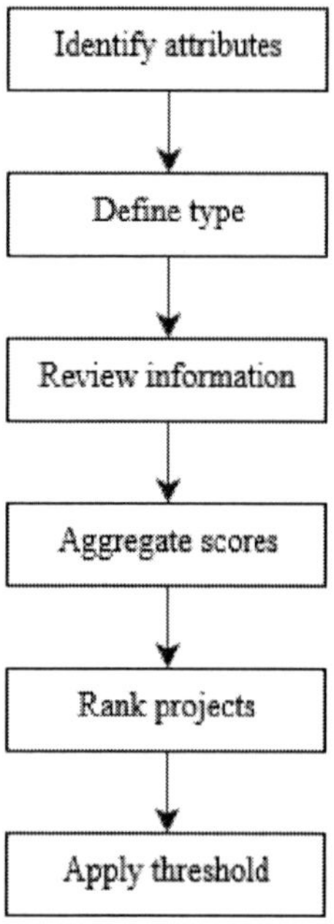

Figure 11. Portfolio Management process stages

The ABC Threshold approach process shown in Figure 11 highlights the simplicity of utilizing this as a method to investigate, evaluate and prioritise a company's portfolio. This is achieved through identification of important information, capturing it, reviewing that which is captured, collecting scores and comparing to a defined threshold to identify the development project to proceed with, if any.

IV. Discussion and Conclusion

The ABC Threshold approach outlined above has several advantages. Firstly, the same attributes from different potential development projects can be directly compared after conversion into a numerical form on the same Normalised Scale. This can deliver an understanding of where certain developments are stronger than others. Secondly, it is very flexible for the company, as any attribute can be scored using the outlined methods. Therefore only the information that is important to the company is analysed. The approach also diminishes the impact of subjectivity on the final score. By defining the review process to be one of three methods, the results found from different points of view should be very similar; meaning the consistent results can be achieved irrespective of who is conducting the review. Bias and personal influence can also be minimised as the final score is not created on the basis of discussion but rather the generation of numerical scores. Finally, the process is reflective of the company's position, as the decision threshold value can be set at the appropriate level. For companies with limited resources, such as small and medium sized enterprises [1], this threshold level can be increased such that potential development projects have to display a higher level of certainty of success before committing to them.

Overall, the ABC Threshold approach can be thought of as a structured investigation, evaluation and prioritisation tool.

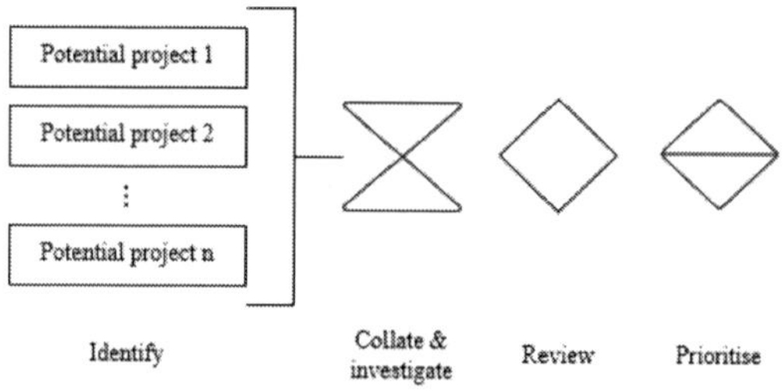

Figure 12. Portfolio Management process

As can be seen in Figure 12, potential development projects are identified, collated and investigated, reviewed and then prioritised. From this prioritisation of potential development projects, resources can be distributed as required. Furthermore, additional investigations can be initiated for those potential development projects that fall short of the required threshold. Brand new potential development projects can also be considered at this stage to increase the chance of identifying viable projects.

To manage multiple potential and actual development projects, Portfolio Management is used. Numerous tools, method and frameworks have been devised that aid in the investigation, evaluation and prioritisation. This is vital when distributing resources to those prospective projects that have the greatest potential. Many existing tools, methods and frameworks commonly focus on monetary attributes or only use a fixed set; those approaches can be very inflexible and not truly reflective of what is important to the particular company. The proposed ABC Threshold approach to Portfolio Management allows for customisation by the company to the attributes that are most important to describe a potential development project. In addition, clear indications as to the development path to follow are given by the use of the threshold approach which can also indicate when additional investigation is required.

However there are several possible considerations related to the ABC Threshold approach. Within a company setting, a system to implement the three methods is required; this would necessitate the correct development and error checking. Secondly, the required data needs storing in a way that is easily collected for utilisation in the scoring methods. Finally, as noted earlier, the set threshold can have a profound impact on the potential developments selected. Therefore the setting of the level is critical and will require careful consideration and potentially trial and error to correctly match the given situation.

In summary, the ABC Threshold approach gives enough flexibility to the company to adopt bespoke Portfolio Management by identifying the attributes that are most important to them for investigation and evaluation whilst being non-subjective, devoid of bias and delivering a true reflection of the company's R&D position via adoption of an appropriate decision threshold value.

ACKNOWLEDGMENT

This work was supported by the Systems Centre and the EPSRC funded Industrial Doctorate Centre in Systems (Grant EP/G037353/1) and Imetrum Limited.

REFERENCES

[1] R. McAdam, R. Reid, and M. Shevlin, "Determinants for innovation implementation at SME and inter SME levels within peripheral regions," *Int. J. Entrep. Behav. Res.*, vol. 20, no. 1, pp. 66–90, 2014.

[2] M. Abbassi, M. Ashrafi, and E. Sharifi Tashnizi, "Selecting balanced portfolios of R&D projects with interdependencies: A cross-entropy based methodology," *Technovation*, vol. 34, no. 1, pp. 54–63, 2014.

[3] A. D. Henriksen and A. J. Traynor, "A practical R & D project-selection scoring tool," *{IEEE} Trans. Eng. Manag.*, vol. 46, no. 2, pp. 158–170, 1999.

[4] R. C. McNally, S. S. Durmuşoğlu, and R. J. Calantone, "New product portfolio management decisions: Antecedents and consequences," *J. Prod. Innov. Manag.*, vol. 30, no. 2, pp. 245–261, 2013.

[5] P. Patanakul, "Key drivers of effectiveness in managing a group of multiple projects," *IEEE Trans. Eng. Manag.*, vol. 60, no. 1, pp. 4–17, 2013.

[6] R. Sperry and A. Jetter, "Theoretical framework for managing the front end of innovation under uncertainty," *PICMET Portl. Int. Cent. Manag. Eng. Technol. Proc.*, pp. 2021–2028, 2009.

[7] M. G. Kaiser, F. El Arbi, and F. Ahlemann, "Successful project portfolio management beyond project selection techniques: Understanding the role of structural alignment," *Int. J. Proj. Manag.*, vol. 33, no. 1, pp. 126–139, 2015.

[8] M. Martinsuo, "Project portfolio management in practice and in context," *Int. J. Proj. Manag.*, vol. 31, no. 6, pp. 794–803, 2013.

[9] R. Mitchell, R. Phaal, and N. Athanassopoulou, "Scoring methods for prioritizing and selecting innovation projects," *PICMET 2014 - Portl. Int. Cent. Manag. Eng. Technol. Proc. Infrastruct. Serv. Integr.*, no. 2001, pp. 907–920, 2014.

[10] Q. Tian, J. Ma, J. Liang, R. C. W. Kwok, and O. Liu, "An organizational decision support system for effective R&D project selection," *Decis. Support Syst.*, vol. 39, no. 3, pp. 403–413, 2005.

[11] H. Eilat, B. Golany, and A. Shtub, "Constructing and evaluating balanced portfolios of R&D projects with interactions: A DEA based methodology," *Eur. J. Oper. Res.*, vol. 172, no. 3, pp. 1018–1039, 2006.

[12] S. Coldrick, P. Longhurst, P. Ivey, and J. Hannis, "An R&D options selection model for investment decisions," *Technovation*, vol. 25, no. 3, pp. 185–193, 2005.

[13] K. Katz and T. Manzione, "Maximize Your 'Return on Initiatives' with the Initiative Portfolio Review Process," *Haarvard Bus. Rev.*, pp. 14–16, 2008.

[14] J. Cho and J. Lee, "Development of a new technology product evaluation model for assessing commercialization opportunities using Delphi method and fuzzy AHP approach," *Expert Syst. Appl.*, vol. 40, no. 13, pp. 5314–5330, 2013.

[15] R. Roy, S. Colmer, and T. Griggs, "Estimating the Cost of a New Technology Intensive Automotive Product: A Case Study Approach," *Int. J. Prod. Econ.*, vol. 97, no. 2, pp. 210–226, 2005.

[16] D. R. Lairson, T. H. Chung, L. G. Smith, J. K. Springston, and V. L. Champion, "Estimating development cost of an interactive website based cancer screening promotion program," *Eval. Program Plann.*, vol. 50, pp. 56–62, 2015.

[17] E. H. Forman. and S. I. Gass, "The Analytic Hierarchy Process--An Exposition," *Oper. Res.*, vol. 49, no. 4, pp. 469–486, 2001.

[18] A. Omid and S. H. Zegordi, "Integrated AHP and network DEA for assessing the efficiency of Iranian handmade carpet industry," *Decis. Sci. Lett.*, vol. 4, no. 4, pp. 477–486, 2015.

[19] R. Ramanathan and L. S. Ganesh, "Using AHP for resource allocation problems," *Eur. J. Oper. Res.*, vol. 80, no. 93, pp. 410–417, 1995.

[20] C. Raspotnig and A. Opdahl, "Comparing risk identification techniques for safety and security requirements," *J. Syst. Softw.*, vol. 86, no. 4, pp. 1124–1151, 2013.

[21] D. Guégan and X. Zhao, "Alternative modeling for long term risk," *Quant. Financ.*, vol. 7688, no. December 2013, pp. 1–17, 2013.

AUTHOR INDEX